KID KOWBOYS

JUVENILES IN WESTERN FILMS

by

Bob Nareau

Published by:

Empire Publishing, Inc.
PO Box 717
Madison, NC 27025-0717

Phone: 336-427-5850 • Fax: 336-427-7372
www.empirepublishinginc.com

As if being one of Hollywood's leading "Kid Kowboys" and a highly-decorated veteran of two wars was not enough fame, Sammy McKim went on to become an acclaimed artist. This book's cover is an original Sam McKim work of art. We express our grateful thanks, Sam. Readers will treasure your contribution.

TABLE OF CONTENTS

ACKNOWLEDGMENTS

A book of this scope would have been an impossible task without the aid of many friends, acquaintances, and institutions. Thus, to the following I express my heartfelt thanks for the role they played in bringing this project to fruition.

BOBBY COPELAND, friend and fellow author, for suggesting additional names to be included, many of whom I had long forgotten—or had never heard of—along with other contributions.

BOYD MAGERS, good friend and the editor of that super publication, *Western Clippings*, who offered encouragement, provided names and material, and established contacts.

BILL RUSSELL, friend, author, and western researcher, for his many contributions.

LUTHER HATHCOCK, friend, author, and the man I call the "Sam Spade" of B-western research, for his ability to ferret out information on some of the difficult-to-locate western players.

JANET LORENZ, Academy of Motion Picture Arts and Sciences, who located and provided hard-to-find material.

THE INTERNET MOVIE DATA BASE for filmographies and dates.

THE CALIFORNIA BUREAU OF VITAL STATISTICS for information provided.

JACK MATHIS of Jack Mathis Advertising, special thanks for a select group of photos supplied to enhance the quality of this book.

And to those whose material I have used, brains I have picked, and who have been but a phone call away for advice, requests, or answers:

Lee Aaker
Rex Rossi
Les Adams
Billy Gray
Gary Gray
Jimmy Hawkins
The late Nick Nicholls
Bill Sasser
The family of Newton and Jimmy House

Michael Fitzgerald
The late Ed Wyatt
Dick Jones
Jimmy Hunt
Teddy Infuhr
Tommy Ivo
Tom Nichols
Sonny Bupp
Harry McKim
Sam McKim
Fred Sale, Jr.
Beverly Washburn
Michael Chapin
Eilene Janssen
Tommy Cook
Johnny Duncan

To my lovely wife, Greta Nareau, for running all the errands associated with putting a book together, and for every task necessary to the operations of my computer, other than my two-fingered typing, as I am the first to admit that I am computer illiterate.

And to my granddaughter, Madaline "Punky" Nareau for keeping me young.

The "KID," Madaline "Punky" Nareau, with "Kid Kowboys" left to right: Michael Chapin, Eilene Janssen, Tommy Cook, Teddy Infuhr, and Gary Gray.

Author's Comment: Who better to write a foreword for a book about "Kid Kowboys" than someone who has "been there, done that"? Thanks, Gary.

FOREWORD

I cannot begin to tell you how honored I am to have been asked by Bob Nareau to do the Foreword for this book on the kids who worked in westerns, during what I would call the golden years of the motion picture industry, and the days of the B-western. You remember when the good guys wore white hats, the bad guys always wore black hats, and good always won over bad. I know you will enjoy this book, and will not only find out a lot about your favorite "Kid Kowboys" while they were working in the motion picture industry, but what has happened to them as they grew up and went on with their lives.

I was lucky enough to have been one of those kids, and to me it was a wonderful life! How lucky could you get? I was living in Los Angeles and grew up playing cowboys and Indians, emulating my heroes that I went to see at the Hitching Post Theater (where we had to check our cap guns before we went in) on Saturday afternoons. Being fortunate enough to have been working in pictures, I was able to go to the studio and actually work with—and know—my heroes. I also got to meet a lot of other stars even though I did not get to work with them.

There always seem to be a lot of questions that come up regarding kids who worked in the motion picture industry: Did you have a normal childhood? What was school like at the studio? What happened to the money you made while working as an actor? And last, but not least, is how come you grew up and led a normal life while so many others had problems with drugs, going to jail, etc? I will try to address these issues so you will know what it was like growing up in the motion picture industry.

First off, I have to tell you that the vast majority of children who grew up making movies turned out just fine. I know, because I remain friends with quite a few of them. They went on to become doctors, lawyers, computer wizards, schoolteachers, and salesmen (I was the national sales manager for a major manufacturer in the swimming pool industry, my chosen profession for almost 40 years). Many of the child stars even stayed in the movie industry, becoming well known for their work behind the camera as well as in front of it. In fact, the careers they chose cover everything from A to Z. Most importantly, they became good, loving mothers and fathers. It has always been my belief that those who got into trouble would have managed to get into trouble, no matter what their occupation was. It would have made no difference if they had been selling newspapers, or had been a doctor, lawyer, or Indian chief.

If you were working on a motion picture, you were required to have three hours of schooling a day. The schoolteacher was also a welfare worker, and he/she made sure you got your three hours of schooling, plus one hour for lunch, and that you did not work in front of the camera for more than four hours per day. Sometimes you were lucky and could get all of your schooling finished by the time lunch came around, but the chances were that you would get your schooling in fifteen or thirty-minute increments, and sometimes, even smaller increments. While some of the kids did not think they received a very good education, I never felt that way; after all, for the most part it was one-on-one with the teacher. I was lucky enough to be in a position where we could request certain teachers, and my folks always made sure the teachers they requested were the best.

Most of the kids, when they were not working, went to public schools, while some went to private schools. If you were under term contract at a studio, you went to school at the studio (even if you were not working on a picture) with the other kids who were under contract at that studio. During my career I did all three, because for most of my career I was what was known as a freelance actor. I worked at all of the studios either with single or multiple-picture contracts. I attended public school until the fourth grade, and then I went to Hollywood Professional School. It was a school designed for the children who worked in pictures (the school day was from 8 A.M. until noon), because it left afternoons free for interviews, dancing, singing, or drama lessons. Actually, there were more kids there who wanted to be in pictures than were in pictures. Many parents just thought their children could get a better education there than they could get at a public school. In fact, that was the main reason my folks had me go there. I remained at Hollywood Professional School until I was put under term contract at MGM. When my contract was terminated, I went back to public school, attending Van Nuys Jr. and Sr. High. While at Van Nuys High, I lettered in varsity diving and gymnastics, competing in the long horse, side horse, parallel bars, tumbling, free exercise and would sometimes fill in on the high bar. I belonged to a car club (The Stylers) and did everything else like the rest of the kids. Did I have a "normal" life? You *bet!* My mother and father saw to that. I might have been working at the studio during the week, but if I wanted spending money, I mowed lawns up and down the street. My folks wanted to make sure that I grew up with everyday values.

Another thing we hear a lot about is parents who spent all the money that their child made. I know this has happened; however, I think a lot of the kids forget the expense that is incurred—both financially and personally—by their parents. I know there was not a day that I was working that my mother (or father, if he could break away from his business) was not on the set with me. At night, my mother or father would run lines with me for the next day's shooting. If I was working on a picture, my sister had to be at a private day care or she had to have a sitter, and of course there was private schooling and dancing lessons for her, also. If I was working, there was little time for anything else, so we would have a cleaning person during that period. And don't forget Uncle Sam; he always gets his share as did the talent agent, publicity man, and possibly a business manager (I was lucky there, as my dad was a business manager for many of the stars in Hollywood). There were also clipping services, autograph services, and the list goes on. To say the least, there are lots of expenses, and I have only named a few.

I often hear child actors say they feel they have been cheated out of their childhood and/or their earnings by their parents. Personally I never even thought of acting as work, or that I was ever cheated out of anything; I was having a ball! I think these kids have forgotten how much time, work, and effort their parents put into helping them become a child star. They also say they were the main bread winner of the family, and that their father or mother did not like being introduced as the father or mother of the child star. They say it made the parents feel inferior in some way. That sure wasn't the case in our family. I know there were years that I did better financially than my father, but he was always the patriarch of our family. There was never a misunderstanding about that. I think a lot depends on the parents. Not only in how they brought up their child, but in how the parents looked at their own self worth and their feeling of security. Personally, my mom and dad always got a kick out of it when they were introduced as my parents. In fact, it even made them proud.

How anyone could not like growing up working in pictures I will never know. It was really a great experience! At the time I was doing a lot of the westerns, we were living in an apartment, and I could not even have a dog. But, I could go to the studio or go out on location and ride horses or drive a team. I worked with every dog (from Daisy to Flame and Lassie) that was in pictures at the time. In fact, when we moved out of the apartment, I wound up with one of Lassie's puppies (Laddie) as my dog. As I got a little older, I had a horse and learned how to trick ride. What a GREAT LIFE! If I could do it all over again I would. I know the things I learned while working in pictures have helped me all through my life, and I am still benefiting from those experiences today.

Thanks, Bob, for your friendship and the opportunity of sharing with your readers what it was like being a "Kid Kowboy," and growing up working in the motion picture industry.

—Gary Gray

DEDICATION

I pondered long hours about to whom this book should be dedicated.

Since the book is about kids and cowboys, I harkened back to those halcyon days when I was a kid, and the cowboys were not only my—but most kids'—heroes. I thought about those Saturday matinees, when one of the highlights of our young lives was to view our favorite western stars teaching us that good always conquered evil. I reminisced about those glorious days when the dream of every kid was to own a six-shooting cap gun, or a Daisy air rifle, to better spend our leisure hours playing cowboys and Indians. Shouts of "bang, bang, you're dead," pierced the air, and whether on that particular day your role was one of the heroe 'bad guy," or a Cheyenne, the da   s a bonus. Amazingly, all of this gunplay never seemed to continue as an important role in our lives as the years went by. I can't think of a single instance when any of those kids later in life used a weapon to illegally take a human life or to commit a criminal deed. Our fascination with guns eroded as we were off on new pursuits and discovered other interests, like baseball and girls.

In today's world, parent-teacher groups, concerned adults, the "politically correct," and psychologists have deemed that toy guns are prone to inducing a life of violence. Hence, toy six-guns are a verboten relic of the past and "cowboys and Indians" are no longer one of the joys of being a kid. Kids grow up, parental and adult influences wane, and "political correctness" is something many of these kids could care less about. Resentments germinate, and the cap pistol that was "forbidden fruit" becomes the desire for the "real thing." Kids shoot kids over an invasion of their "turf." Kids shoot up their schools. Kids use guns to get whatever strikes their fancy. What was once a permitted and acceptable fantasy becomes a deadly way of life. Perhaps it's time to let kids be kids again. Perhaps it's time for Hollywood to reinvent the B-western, and for the "politically correct" to crawl into a hole. Perhaps it's time to say, "Momma, it's all right to let your babies grow up to be cowboys."

Thus, a tip of the sombrero to some who are providing us with the way to keep the dreams of those joyous days of our youth alive: Boyd and Donna Magers, and George Coan.

BOYD AND DONNA MAGERS

Six times each year Boyd and Donna publish *Western Clippings*, a periodical that keeps its readers

informed of happenings—past, present, and future—in the lives of cinema's western heroes, heroines, heavies and role players. There are feature articles, medical up-dates, obituaries, television news, book reviews, film festival notices, photos, and numerous columns in each issue dealing with every aspect of the western film. The bulk mail subscription rate is a mere $23.40 per year, or $27.50 for first class delivery. Fans can subscribe by contacting Boyd or Donna at 1312 Stagecoach Road S.E., Albuquerque, New Mexico 87123, (505) 292-0049, or by e-mail (vidwest@abq.net).

Donna and Boyd Magers

GEORGE COAN

Every other month, George mails out *The Old Cowboy Picture Show*, an informative newsletter of several pages that keeps western fans informed of a myriad of items relating to the B-westerns. There are festival updates, feature articles, photos, correspondence, and western trivia. George is also behind a program each month that puts on a Saturday matinee reminiscent of the days of our youth, and don't worry if you can't find a dime—it's free. One of the great things about George's

newsletter is that it is also free, although donations are accepted to help defray the considerable mailing expense. Send your donation to George at P.O. Box 66, Camden, South Carolina 29020; get on the mailing list; and once again, recall and enjoy those years when "terror" was worrying whether or not you could find an extra nickel for some penny candy to take you through those great Saturday afternoons.

George is ably assisted in the production of this welcome project by his loyal sidekick, Leo Pando. Leo does most of his contributions as editor, designer and producer from his seven-acre "ranch" in Maine.

George and Leo together at the 2001 Western Film Festival at Charlotte, North Carolina.

INTRODUCTION

Remember those great Saturday afternoon "shoot 'em ups," when for a dime we could get to watch "the big picture," the "chapter," a comedy and a cartoon, and for a nickel more we could buy enough jaw breakers and other assorted candy to last throughout the show?

Recall the thrills and screams of delight at the ridin', ropin', shootin', and fightin' as Bob Steele, Ken Maynard, Buck Jones, and a myriad of our other heroes took care of the "bad guys"?

Recall the giggles and guffaws at the antics of Gabby Hayes, Al St. John and "Fuzzy" Knight as they helped our heroes tame the west?

Recall our disdain for the men in the black hats—Dick Curtis, Charlie King and Jack Ingram—as they tried to do harm to the "good guys"?

Recall the chills as we watched Rin Tin Tin, Strongheart, Tarzan, Silver, and Rex, king of the wild horses, perform their magic as they helped bring justice to the range?

Recall our secret loves, that we would not discuss with even our best friends, with those beautiful heroines: Myrna Dell, Harley Wood, and Arletta Duncan?

But, can you recall the envy we felt as we watched youngsters of our own age group fortunate to be sharing the silver screen with our idols and helping restore law and order to the wild west?

A few of these lucky juvenile cowboys and cowgirls—such as Frankie Darro, Buzz Barton, and Dickie Jones—were with us often at the matinee, and even went on to long and rewarding films careers. Others, we saw but rarely—a role here or there—but seldom, if ever, seen or heard from again.

We know the answer to "What Ever Happened to Randolph Scott?" But many of us are still seeking to find out what happened to Newton House, Mickey Rentschler, Bobby Nelson, Freddie Mercer, Bennie Bartlett, Annabelle Magnus, and a host of others who wore boots and spurs and rode horses while we were wearing Keds and riding bicycles.

Let the search begin.

Note: The qualify as a "Kid Kowboy," the performer must have appeared in one or more Western films prior to reaching 18 years of age.

The Internet Movie Data Base (IMBD) provides for interesting reading, and is somewhat valuable as a research tool. However, it should not be considered totally factual due to its many errors.

LEE AAKER

While his juvenile roles in big screen westerns are limited, Lee Aaker gained a certain measure of fame in the role of "Corporal Rusty," the lone survivor of an Apache raid, who was adopted by a cavalry unit in the television series "The Adventures of Rin Tin Tin" (1954-59).

Lee William Aaker was born on September 25, 1943, in Inglewood, California. Lee's father, DeForrest Aaker, was a construction worker. from South Dakota. His mother, Dorothe, was from Detroit and ran a tap dance school. Lee says his parents divorced early on, and after his mother remarried, his stepfather, Miles Webous, an accountant who was from Minnesota, became the father figure in the Aaker home. Lee has an older brother, Dee. A note of interest: one of Lee's grandfathers was a championship swimmer in the Shetland Islands.

Aaker's early education was at Columbia Studios' school where one of his classmates and best friends was actor Paul Petersen. Lee went on to graduate from Inglewood High School and was also a member of the California Air National Guard.

Lee's entry into films was at the age of four in what appears to be a short subject, THE GOVER-NOR OF LOUISIANA ('47). He is credited in BENJY ('51), possibly another short subject. His first full-length picture was THE GREATEST SHOW ON EARTH ('52) starring James Stewart and Betty Hutton. Lee's final film credit was BYE BYE BIRDIE ('63) supporting Janet Leigh and Ann Margaret. In those interim years he made appearances in O. HENRY'S FULL HOUSE ('52) a film with such stars as Fred Allen, Anne Baxter and Marilyn Monroe. Lee played the role of "Red Chief" in the segment of the film devoted to William Sidney Porter's delightful short story, THE RANSOM OF RED CHIEF. Other films in this era are MISTER SCOUTMASTER ('53), ARENA ('53), with Gig Young, TAKE ME TO TOWN ('53) with Ann Sheridan, RICOCHET ROMANCE ('54) with Marjorie Main and Chill Wills, DESTRY ('54), with Audie Murphy, SPIN AND MARTY: THE MOVIE ('55), BIGGER THAN LIFE ('56) and THE CHALLENGE OF RIN TIN TIN ('57), which was compiled from "Rin Tin Tin" television episodes.

Lee's only true western role during his brief Hollywood days was his appearance with John Wayne in HONDO ('53). He made guest appearances on television shows, including "The Lone Ranger," "Screen Directors Playhouse," "The Loretta Young Show," and "The Danny Thomas Show." He served as assistant producer during the television series "Route 66."

Lee has been twice married and has no children. When asked about his ex-wives, he, understandably, preferred not to discuss them. His best friend, Paul Petersen, was the best man at one of Lee's trips down the aisle.

Over a period of years, during his adult life, Lee suffered from anxiety and panic attacks during public appearances. He became pretty much a recluse as the problem was not diagnosed or treated. (Good friend, Jim Bradbury, the younger brother of western star Bob Steele, served with General Patton during World War II. Jim was wounded in action and decorated for his service. He also was, at one time, a victim of the same attacks. Jim remarked if he could make a choice between anxiety or panic attacks and being on the front line with bombs exploding and bullets flying, his preference would be the hazards of war. Fortunately, both Lee and Jim now have this medical problem under control.) Unfortunately, it was during this period of Aaker's life that a despicable imposter represented himself at numerous public functions as being the real Lee Aaker. Many people were defrauded into paying money for false autographs and photos, and airfare and accommodations to meet this pseudo celebrity. However, recently Lee (working in tandem with friend and fellow actor Paul Petersen and Boyd Magers exposed the phony and put an end to his nefarious scheme.

Following his acting career, Aaker became an independent building contractor but says he is basically retired now. Lee Aaker is an outdoorsman. He is an avid snow and water skier and loves hiking the wilderness trails. To understand what kind of person he is, Lee recently confirmed to the author how he spends his spare time: "I teach handicapped ski school in the winter. I teach blind kids and kids with one leg and other disadvantages to snow ski. I've been a skier all my life. I read an article about two or three years ago concerning the need for volunteers to help kids learn to ski. That's how I got started."

Lee's favorite actor is John Wayne, with whom he appeared in HONDO. He also spoke highly of Tony Curtis with whom he had a supporting role in NO ROOM FOR THE GROOM ('52). He says that his favorite role was that of "Red Chief" in O. HENRY'S FULL HOUSE.

Lee now resides in the beautiful Mammoth Lakes area of California and is ready to return as a guest at western film festivals.

WALLY ALBRIGHT

Six of the fifty-some film credits amassed by juvenile player Wally Albright are in "Kid Kowboy" roles.

Born Walton Algernon Albright, Jr. on September 3, 1925, in Burbank, California, he was the son of a Minnesota-born father and Lois Ethelynn Coward of Tennessee. Sometimes billed as Wallace Albright and other times as Wally Albright, Jr., he made his film debut in THE CASE OF LENA SMITH ('29). Like many of the juvenile players of those days, Wally was an early member of the "Our Gang" comedy group, appearing in six of the popular short subjects.

Albright's western films consisted of roles in THE CONQUERORS ('32) with Richard Dix and Ann Harding, END OF THE TRAIL ('32) with Tim McCoy, THE COWBOY STAR ('36) with Charles Starrett, OLD LOUISIANA ('37) with Tom Keene and Rita Cansino (later to become Rita Hayworth), ROLL ALONG, COWBOY ('37) with Smith Ballew, and MEXICALI ROSE ('39) with Gene Autry and "Smiley" Burnette.

Some of the more notable films and players Wally supported include THUNDER ('29) with Lon Chaney, THE SINGLE STANDARD ('29) with Greta Garbo, THE TRESPASSER ('29) with Gloria Swanson, LAW OF THE SEA ('31) with William Farnum and Rex Bell, THIRTEEN WOMEN ('32) with Irene Dunne and Myrna Loy, ZOO IN BUDAPEST ('33) with Loretta Young, MR. SKITCH ('33) with Will Rogers and Zasu Pitts, THE WRECKER ('33) with Jack Holt, THE COUNT OF MONTE CRISTO ('34) with Robert Donat, KID MILLIONS ('34) with Eddie Cantor, O'SHAUGHNESSY'S BOY ('35) with Wallace Beery and Jackie Cooper, BLACK FURY ('35) with Paul Muni, LITTLE MISS NOBODY ('36) with Jane Withers, MAID OF SALEM ('37) Claudette Colbert and Fred MacMurray, CAPTAINS COURAGEOUS ('37) with Spencer Tracy. SONS OF THE LEGION ('38) with Donald O'Connor and Billy Lee, THE GRAPES OF WRATH ('40) with Henry Fonda, and JOHNNY APOLLO ('40) with Tyrone Power and Dorothy Lamour. Albright's last film credit was an un-credited role as a cyclist in Marlon Brando's THE WILD ONE ('54).

Wally is credited with 12 years of formal education. During World War II, he served in the U. S. Navy. He was married to Helen Virginia Mathany and the couple had one child, a son Walton Algernon Albright II. The Albrights made their home in Carlsbad, California.

Following his film career, Wally operated his own produce packing, shipping and trucking business, and invested successfully in real estate. He owned and flew his own plane and was active in a number of leisure pursuits, winning hundreds of trophies in golf, motorcycling, and calf roping. In 1957 he was the men's national champion as a trick skier.

Wally passed away August 7, 1999, while in Sacramento, California. He was hospitalized for four days at Mercy General Hospital before his death. The multiple causes of his demise at age 73 are listed as cardiogenic shock, myocardial infarction, atherosclerotic heart disease, hypertension and chronic obstructive pulmonary disease. His wife and son were among his survivors. Wally lies at rest at Forest Lawn Memorial Park in Glendale, California.

ARMIDA

Armida was born Armida Vendrell in Sonora, Mexico, on either May 29, 1913, or on March 29, 1911. Her father, Joaquin Vendrell, was a well-known stage actor who coached her, along with her five sisters and two brothers, in theater arts. Her father was born in Spain, and her mother, Maria Camlich, was born in Mexico. The family moved from Mexico to Arizona, then on to Los Angeles during Armida's early childhood. While in her teenage years, Armida was performing in a dancing act with two of her sisters when Gus Edwards signed her to a contract and took her to New York. There she was given a part in a vaudeville act, "Ritz Carleton" with Ray Bolger and Lola Lane. Reports state Armida was a huge hit.

Despite her busy schedule, Armida completed 12 years of formal education. In the late 1920s, she returned to Hollywood and made her debut in a series of short films. Photos and reports from those who knew her show Armida to be a beautiful person with a sparkling personality. Small in stature, she was less than five feet tall and weighed less than 100 pounds.

Armida's western film credits while still a juvenile are all during the 1929-1930 era where she had roles in ON THE BORDER with John Litel and Rin Tin Tin, BORDER ROMANCE with Don Terry, and UNDER A TEXAS MOON with Frank Fay. During this period she was "discovered" by John Barrymore, who signed her for an appearance in his film, GENERAL CRACK ('30). During that same year she had a role with another of the early B-western stars, Rex Lease, in WINGS OF ADVENTURE ('30)

Armida was a multi-talented performer. She excelled as a dancer and as a comic. Following her early film experiences, she worked on stage and in radio. Sigmund Romberg's "Nina Rose" was but one of a series of stage successes. She was on radio with Rudy Vallee and Abe Lyman and later starred on her own program. By 1933 she was back in Hollywood with roles—not only in westerns—but also in comedies, drama, and jungle movies. In several of these films Armida had the opportunity to display another talent, her singing ability.

Armida's adult-age westerns included UNDER THE PAMPAS MOON ('35) with Warner Baxter and Rita Casino (later to become Rita Hayworth), ROOTIN' TOOTIN' RHYTHM ('37) with Gene Autry, BORDER CAFE ('37) with Harry Carey, SOUTH OF THE RIO GRANDE ('45) with Duncan Renaldo, BAD MEN OF THE BORDER ('46) with Kirby Grant, and GAY AMIGO ('49) with Duncan Renaldo and Leo Carrillo.

Armida also appeared in the 15-episode, 1948 serial, CONGO BILL ('48) which starred Don McGuire, who later became a talented writer, penning TOOTSIE and other films, and leading lady, Cleo Moore, referred to by one reviewer as a "B movie floozy." Armida's final film appearance was in 1951's RHYTHM INN, which starred Jane Frazee and Kirby Grant. Her role was that of a specialty dancer, and she was credited with composing the dance routines in the film.

A note of interest: while interviewing Rex Rossi, Hollywood stuntman and the screen double for Bob Steele, Rex volunteered that his first wife was Mexican actress, Armida. He stated further that there were two daughters born of this union. Asked if either of the daughters were in show business, Rex replied, "No, thank God."

Armida Vendrell died on October 23, 1989, at the age of 78. Although born in Mexico, at the time of her death, she was a citizen of the United States. Armida's occupation was listed as a self-employed actress and entertainer—she spent 55 years in the entertainment world. Her marital status at the date of her death was divorced. Her place of residence for the last 15 years of her life was 8020 Alston Avenue, Hesperia, San Bernardino County, California. The state of California was informed of the vital statistics of Armida's death by one of her sisters, Lydia Dolan. She died at Victor Valley Community Hospital in Victorville, California, from cardiopulmonary arrest, which occurred within a matter of minutes after days of acute mycardial infarction. Armida Vendrell lies at rest in Victor Valley Memorial Park at 17150 "C" Street, Victorville, California.

WESLEY BARRY

With a Hollywood career that spanned over fifty years and encompassed several avenues within the industry, Wesley Barry managed to appear in four westerns as a "Kid Kowboy." Two of Wesley's westerns are BOB HAMPTON OF PLACER ('21) with James Kirkwood and HIS OWN LAW ('24), where Barry is credited as the lead. He also made two other westerns. He supported Armida and Don Terry in BORDER ROMANCE ('29) and had a good role in MEXICALI KID ('38) with Jack Randall.

Wesley Earl Barry was born on August 10, 1907, in Los Angeles. Barry married and was the father of at least one child—a son, Wesley Earl Barry, II.

Barry's 57 credited actor appearances commenced in the Mary Pickford film, REBECCA OF SUNNYBROOK FARM ('17), and ended with an un-credited role in LADIES' DAY ('23). Interspersed between these two are credits in such "little noted, nor long remembered" offerings as HOW COULD YOU, JEAN? ('18), WOMAN OF PLEASURE ('19), INNOCENTS OF PARIS ('29), THE LIFE OF VERGIE WINTERS ('34), LADY BE CAREFUL ('36), and MR. DOODLE KICKS OFF ('38).

During World War II, Barry spent the years 1942-45 in the U.S. Navy. Returning to Hollywood after the war, Barry went to work on the other side of the camera. He served in the capacity of production assistant, production manager, second unit director, producer, and director in a myriad of films until the early 1970s.

Among the many western films on which Wes worked are BUFFALO BILL RIDES AGAIN, BELLE STARR'S DAUGHTER, TRAIL OF THE YUKON and TRAIL BLAZERS. His television productions included a compilation of several episodes of the "Adventures of Wild Bill Hickok," including made-for-television westerns SIX GUN DECISION, SECRET OF OUTLAW FLATS, BORDER CITY RUSTLERS, OUTLAW'S DAUGHTER, THE TITLED TENDERFOOT, and PHANTOM TRAILS, and the series "Yuma" and "The Rookies."

Wes also worked briefly as a writer. He is credited with the script for RACING BLOOD ('54) and THE JOLLY GENIE ('63). Following his Hollywood retirement, perhaps in memory of some of his early films, he operated a turkey ranch.

Barry passed away on April 11, 1994, at age 86, in Clovis, California. The certificate of death contains the following information: He had 13 years of formal education, and he was widowed at the time of his death. His employer was Aaron Spelling Productions, a television production company, and his usual occupation was listed as a film director of 40 years. Barry's death was reported by Wesley E. Barry, II, his son, with whom he had been residing. There was no mention of other surviving relatives. The stated causes of Wesley Barry's death are legion. They include chronic urinary tract infection, diabetes, cerebro vascular accident, respiratory failure, which Barry suffered only a few hours, probable pneumonia for days, chronic obstructive pulmonary disease for years, and tobacco abuse for decades. Wes Barry's remains were cremated, and lie at rest at Turlock Memorial Park in Turlock, California.

BENNIE BARTLETT

Benny Bartlett (who was also sometimes credited as Bennie Bartlett, Ronnie Bartlett, and David Bartlett) was not only one of Hollywood's most popular young actors, but one of the busiest.

Contrary to what is widely reported, Floyd Benjamin Bartlett was not born in Independence, Kansas, on August 16, 1927, but on August 16, 1924, somewhere in the state of Texas. His parents, Floyd and Nina Bartlett, were performers and part of a traveling show when Benny was born. It's reported for the first three months of Benny's life, his "home" was a trunk in his parents' dressing rooms.

Like much of the information put out by Hollywood regarding the talents of its players, it is sometimes hard to separate fact from fiction. If only a portion of what was offered by Paramount's press releases is true, Benny was somewhat of a rare prodigy. One of the studio early press releases on young Benny reads:

> At the age of two years, Bennie learned to play the drums, and at the age of four, he was actually a trumpet soloist and leader of a professional dance band. It was during this time that the child began to compose music for the lyrics written by Gladys Jolly and Mrs. Mary L. Forbes. Salvatore Santelli and his orchestra featured "The Old Fashioned Mill," which was one of Bennie's compositions. He also composed "With You," "Only Seven," "Georgia Bound," and "You Are So Charming." But Bennie's own favorite of his compositions is "You're Wonderful." He composed the number in tribute to his mother on her wedding anniversary and recently sang it in a radio broadcast.

> The 9-year-old freckled-faced and red-haired youngster has made such a hit that directors and producers are staging a battle royal over him. And the result is that he is so busy that he figuratively meets himself going and coming from the various stages.

> Bennie's parents brought him to Los Angeles in 1932, and he promptly went to work as a trumpet soloist on radio stations. It wasn't long before Paramount Studio executives ordered their talent scouts to bring the boy to the studio. The result was a long-term contract and a lot of work for Bennie.

Another Paramount press release:

> Bennie Bartlett today is convinced that of all the kids lucky enough to get into films he's the luckiest. "Because no other kid needs a job as much as I do," he explains simply. "I'm pinch hitting for Dad for a while," continued the red-haired, freckled-faced 9 year old, "and as the man of the house, I have Mother and three little sisters to support. Dad used to be a soldier, y'know, and the war wasn't so good for him. His health has been failing ever since. He held off going to the hospital as long as he could, because he was the only one in the family earning any money. But he finally had to check in at Sawtelle. Then I got a big part. They made me the rich kid

who makes everyone mad in 13 HOURS BY AIR ('36) but finally helps capture the public enemy. I got my option renewed on account of that and I got my work permit renewed too. Dad's coming along pretty good, too, and soon they say he will be well enough to leave the hospital. But I want to keep on helping him support the kids. I'm beginning to like it."

Another Paramount release soon follows:

Bennie has lost his dog. Featured simultaneously in three Paramount pictures—13 HOURS BY AIR, TIMOTHY'S QUEST ('36), and SKY PARADE ('36)—Bennie is regarded as the find of the decade in the juvenile brackets. Even Fred MacMurray, Joan Bennett, and Zasu Pitts, with whom he is working in 13 HOURS BY AIR, admit that he is stiff competition as an actor. But what good is that if he can't find Ginky Moo, his Japanese lion dog? Ginky Moo is brown and white and answers to her name.

Yet another press release from Paramount letting us all know what's important in Hollywood:

Bennie's father is in the Sawtelle Veteran's hospital. A 15-mile march without breakfast during the World War was so much of a strain that F. A. Bartlett's health was undermined. It has been a ceaseless struggle ever since to regain it. He continues to write arrangements for orchestras broadcasting from KMTR, "The Voice of Hollywood," but his strength is not such that he can work on it constantly.

Ronnie is an earnest little man, not given to clowning off the screen. He's fully conscious of his responsibility. But he gets a lot of pleasure out of miniature airplanes, and his dog, Mr. Towser, who followed his parents home from the corner drugstore one night and got himself adopted. And he still wipes the dishes for his mother. "Cause Dad used to do it," he explains.

(Author's Note: Is this kid for real?)

Next, Paramount informed the world of this important happening in the life of Benny:

Rebelling at the confinement of the classroom, as boys do at intervals the world over, Benny Bartlett and Ra Hould disappeared from the studio school and were gone almost an hour. Investigation by Rachel Smith, their teacher, revealed that it was a premeditated pact. Both boys had brought their roller skates to school with the definite intention of skipping class and going roller skating. While Miss Smith was helping Baby LeRoy with his penmanship in one classroom, Bennie and Ra, a recent importation from Dunedin, New Zealand, slipped out the door of an adjoining classroom with their skates. A search was instituted, and they were collared by a studio policeman about an hour later skimming over the pavements of the studio's New York Street on the back lot. Miss Smith said it was the first case of truancy at the studio school in a long while and punished the boys by keeping them after school.

Then, Paramount let us revel in this exciting news on the life and times of young Mr. Bartlett:

Motorglyding is the latest rage and its addicts are increasing daily. Freckled-faced Bennie Bartlett introduced the pint-sized motorcycle on the Paramount lot, where he persuaded all his young friends to take a whirl on it. Bennie even went so far as to acquire, in some way or another, four of the motorglyders and treated Billie Lee, Jackie Moran and Ra Hould to a spin around the studio lot.

Paramount then let the world know:

One of the west's largest child orchestras has been organized by one of Hollywood's busiest kid actors and is now ready for engagements. This announcement was made by Bennie Bartlett, 12-year-old Paramount player, who between engagements has been able to select the orchestra and direct it with the aid of his father. Bennie has a 16-piece swing ensemble selected from more than 200 applicants. Rehearsals are held twice weekly at the Bartlett house. Just this week they held their first press rehearsal and are now open for dance dates, Bennie says.

Finally, in June of 1937, Paramount issued the following of its press releases available to the author on Bennie Bartlett.

Master Bennie Bartlett, juvenile redhead of the Paramount players' roster, would have the world know that his band of 16 expert musicians is not in competition with other child orchestras. Secondly, Bartlett, Jr., is announcing that his musicians will, within a few weeks, be completely outfitted in powder blue mess jackets and white trousers, with the four girls wearing slacks. The Bartlett band is awaiting an attractive name like Bennie's Band or Bartlett's Wing Gang—something indicating that they are for hot dancers. Bennie's orchestra practices, with permission of neighbors, Saturday mornings and Thursday evenings in his home. They are doing quite well despite the fact that they are trying to unlearn the classics.

There is little doubt Bennie Bartlett was quite talented and was a nice person, but in examining the total picture it appears Bennie, like many, may have been over-hyped. Of his over seventy films, few could be classified as blockbusters. Many of his roles were un-credited, and when he appeared in several of the "Bowery Boys" series, he was in his thirties and hardly a "boy." On loan to 20th Century-Fox, he was showcased as a spoiled, rich boy brought down to earth by Shirley Temple in JUST AROUND THE CORNER ('38). He was cast with Jackie Cooper in the first Henry Aldrich saga, WHAT A LIFE ('39), and in 1939 he had a good role opposite John Barrymore in THE GREAT MAN VOTES.

As for being a "Kid Kowboy," there appear to be only two movies that merit that distinction. In

1936 Bartlett supported Fred MacMurray and Jack Oakie in THE TEXAS RANGERS, and in 1942 he had a good role supporting Bob Steele, Tom Tyler, and Rufe Davis in the "Three Mesquiteers" western, CODE OF THE OUTLAW. His Hollywood career commenced with a piano-playing role in 1935's MILLIONS IN THE AIR and ended either in 1956 with DIG THAT URANIUM (or in 1959's THE SCAPEGOAT, depending on which "historian" one chooses to accept). Bennie is credited with but one television guest appearance, a 1953 episode of "The Cisco Kid." Following his departure from Hollywood, Benny lived in the Santa Barbara, California, area where he was known as Floyd "Ben" Bartlett and worked as an insurance adjuster.

Benny passed away on December 26, 1999, at his home at 1607 St. Andrews Drive in Redding, California, a town in Northern California where Benny had spent the last ten years of his life. The certificate of death confirmed his date of birth as August 16, 1924, and his place of birth was listed as Texas, not Kansas. Benny's death and the statistical information contained in the death certificate was provided by his wife, Mary L. (York) Bartlett. Among the information provided was that Benny had 14 years of education, and his occupation was an actor employed by the film industry, which encompassed a period of 65 years. The certificate further states Benny served in the military, which may explain the hiatus between 1943-1946 in his film appearances.

An odd note to his death certificate is that it contains a space asking whether or not the decedent was of Hispanic origin. The answer in Benny's case was in the affirmative. Both of Benny's parents were born in Kansas. His mother was Nina Timmons, a first name that suggests Hispanic heritage. No information could ascertain whether or not Benny ever fathered children.

Benny Bartlett suffered many health problems prior to his death. The primary cause of his demise was stated as multiple myeloma, a form of bone marrow cancer that had been diagnosed 15 months earlier, with contributing factors that included diabetes, hypertension, and congestive heart failure. Bartlett's remains were cremated.

BUZZ BARTON

Buzz Barton, possibly the most popular of all the "Kid Kowboys," had the distinction of not only appearing in westerns as the young sidekick, but also of being the star in his own series of oaters while still a juvenile. "Buzz" was born William Andrew Lamoreaux on September 3, 1913, in Galatin, Missouri. His family later moved to California and settled in the Newhall area.

Legend has it young Buzz would spend time hanging around the western film sites in Newhall, and it was there he met cowboy star, Jack Perrin, who befriended him and was responsible for getting him into films. Barton and Perrin remained close friends for life. In 1926 Buzz made his screen debut with Tom Tyler in SPLITTING THE BREEZE with Hollywood billing him as "Red Lennox." Barton next appeared as the young sidekick of his friend Jack Perrin in several of Perrin's Rayart westerns such as WEST OF THE RAINBOW'S END ('26), HI-JACKING RUSTLERS ('26), THE LAFFIN' FOOL ('27), and THUNDERBOLT TRACK ('27). During these early films, Buzz acted under the name, "Billy LaMar," a name given him by Perrin.

Later in 1927, there came a final film name change when F.B.O. signed the 14-year-old to a long-term contact to star in his own series of western films under the name by which fans know him best, Buzz Barton. Thus, he became the youngest actor to star in a western series. Buzz starred in fourteen features until his contract was terminated in 1930. Among these films are THE BOY RIDER ('27), THE SLINGSHOT KID ('27), WIZARD OF THE SADDLE ('28), THE LITTLE BUCKAROO ('28), THE PINTO KID ('28), THE FIGHTING REDHEAD ('28), THE BANTAM COWBOY ('28), THE YOUNG WHIRLWIND ('28), ROUGH RIDIN' RED ('28), ORPHAN OF THE SAGE ('38), THE VAGABOND CUB ('29), THE FRECKLED RASCAL ('29), THE LITTLE SAVAGE ('29), and PALS OF THE PRAIRIE ('29).

One of the early Barton films was highly acclaimed by reviewers who were apparently impressed by his horsemanship and acting to the point of referring to him as "a combination of Tom Mix, Ken Maynard, and Fred Thomson." These reviews may have been overzealous, but Barton did appear highly talented in his screen riding and roping. Barton's popularity as a Hollywood cowboy was reason enough for the Daisy Company to issue the Buzz Barton Special Daisy Air Rifle, something every kid wanted to own.

But, a caveat: as in many cases of studios and agents touting their stars, there may have been an overabundance of Hollywood hype in some of the claims made in Barton's behalf. Writers had Buzz performing in rodeos when he was ten years old. Studio sources had him winning national titles as "champion trick rider" and "fancy rider" before his 12th birthday, but national rodeo association sources carry no listing of Barton ever winning any titles or events making the claims highly suspect.

Another of Buzz's 1928 films, ORPHAN OF THE SAGE, written by Oliver Drake, received the following glowing comments: "The boy Indian scout, Buzz Barton, does his acting and his riding in a manner to create the envy of older western stars." The review goes on to applaud the acting of two leading players, a twelve-year-old boy and a twelve-year-old girl. The "twelve-year-old boy" was Buzz *(who was actually 15 at the time, but that's Hollywood)*. The twelve-year-old girl was Annabelle Magnus.

During the next couple of years, Buzz had support roles with many of Hollywood's B-western stars. He appeared in CANYON HAWKS ('30) with Yakima Canutt, BREED OF THE WEST ('30) with Wally Wales, THE APACHE KID'S ESCAPE ('30) and WILD WEST WHOOPEE ('31) both with Jack Perrin, RIDERS OF THE CACTUS 31) and FLYING LARIATS ('31) both with Wally Wales, THE CYCLONE KID ('31) with Caryl Lincoln, and HUMAN TARGETS ('32) with Rin Tin Tin, Jr.

In 1932 film roles were hard to obtain, and Buzz spent the next three years appearing with various circus groups touring the country. After he returned to Hollywood, Buzz supported Rex Bell in a series of four oaters—THE TONTO KID ('34), FIGHTING PIONEERS ('35), SADDLE ACES ('35) and GUNFIRE ('35). Buzz next appeared with a cast that included many of cinema's cowboy heroes in POWDERSMOKE RANGE ('35). Then came THE RECKLESS BUCKAROO ('35) with Bill Cody, THE RIDING AVENGER ('36) with Hoot Gibson, and ROMANCE RIDES THE RANGE ('36) with Fred Scott. Three westerns starring Jack Luden were next in line for the "Bantam Cowboy": ROLLING CARAVANS ('38), STAGECOACH DAYS ('38), and PHANTOM GOLD ('38). Bill Elliott was next to use Buzz in a couple of films, IN EARLY ARIZONA ('38) and LONE STAR PIONEERS ('39). Barton's Hollywood career wound down with support roles in SILVER ON THE SAGE ('39) with William Boyd, WILD HORSE VALLEY ('40) with Bob Steele, and THE KID FROM SANTA FE ('40) with Jack Randall.

Buzz had roles in two, and possibly three, serials. He was with Rin Tin Tin in THE LONE DEFENDER ('30), and in THE MYSTERY TROOPER ('31) with Robert Frazer. In *The Life and Films of Buck Jones—The Sound Era* author Buck Rainey lists Buzz as a cast member in the serial WHITE EAGLE ('41).

Barton did have an unbilled role in THE STORY OF VERNON AND IRENE CASTLE ('39). IMDB credits Buzz with unbilled roles in COME ON DANGER ('42) with Tim Holt, and IN THE HEAT OF THE NIGHT ('67) with Sidney Poitier and Rod Steiger.

Following the attack on Pearl Harbor on December 7, 1941, Buzz joined the U.S. Navy and served in the Pacific theatre during the war. He was a crewmember of the U.S.S. Missouri and was onboard the ship during the signing of the peace agreement that ended the war. Returning to California after the war, his movie career finished, Buzz went into ranching.

On June 22, 1947, Barton married his fiancé, Thelma. The couple moved to Arizona where they later adopted a baby girl named Linda. In 1956 the family returned to the Newhall, California, area where Buzz allegedly worked as a horse wrangler in a number of western films, including THE SHOOTIST, John Wayne's final film. This claim is also suspect. Poor health forced Buzz into retirement in 1979.

On November 20, 1980, the "Bantam Cowboy" passed away at Reseda, California, at age 67. Buzz lies at rest in Eternal Valley Memorial Park in Newhall, California. Barton's widow Thelma, born in 1919, passed away in Los Angeles in February 2000.

NOAH BEERY, JR.

Noah Beery, Jr. was born in New York City on August 10, 1913, the son of actor Noah Beery, Sr. and the senior Beery's first wife, silent actress Marguerita Lindsay. There was another Hollywood connection in Junior's life—his uncle was actor Wallace Beery. Although he had roles in well over 100 films in a career that spanned over sixty years, it was a single movie that qualifies Noah Beery, Jr. as one of the Kid Cowboys. At the age of seven he supported his famous father and Douglas Fairbanks, Sr. in THE MARK OF ZORRO ('20).

Noah's early education was obtained at the Hollywood School for Girls (boys were also admitted). Among his classmates were a couple of other Juniors—Douglas Fairbanks, Jr., and Lon Chaney, Jr. Later, his education consisted of attending Hollywood High School and the Urban and Harvard Military Academies. For much of his youthful years, the family resided in a large home on Vine Street in the middle of Hollywood. While attending the military academies, young Noah found time to appear in stock with his father.

By the time he was nineteen Noah's cinema career was off and running. He supported Tom Tyler in the serial JUNGLE MYSTERY ('32). Then he had the lead in the serial, HEROES OF THE

WEST ('32) with support from veteran western players William Desmond and Edmund Cobb. Other serial roles followed, including FIGHTING WITH KIT CARSON ('33) where he played an Indian and supported Johnny Mack Brown. Included in the cast were his father and juvenile Betsy King Ross. Next in order of his serials was TAILSPIN TOMMY ('34) patterned after the famous comic strip of the same name. Here Noah played second lead and the role of "Skeeter," Tailspin's sidekick. The lead role went to actor Maurice Murphy. His next serial was a starring role with Dorothy Short in CALL OF THE SAVAGE ('35). Among Noah's other serials were TAILSPIN TOMMY IN THE GREAT AIR MYSTERY ('35) with Clark Williams as Tommy and Jean Rogers replacing Patricia Farr as the feminine lead, ACE DRUMMOND ('36) with John "Dusty" King in the lead role, RIDERS OF DEATH VALLEY ('41) with a cast that included Dick Foran, Buck Jones, "Big Boy" Williams, and Monte Blue, and OVERLAND MAIL ('42) with these familiar names in the cast, Lon Chaney, Jr., Helen Parrish, Don Terry, Bob Baker, and Noah Beery, Sr.

Beery played in his first western features during 1933 when he joined Tom Mix in RUSTLERS' ROUNDUP and Randolph Scott in SUNSET PASS. Over the ensuing fifty years some of Noah's more noteworthy movies are roles in the acclaimed OF MICE AND MEN ('39), 20 MULE TEAM ('40), a film where he joined his uncle Wallace Beery, THE CARSON CITY KID ('40) with Roy Rogers and Bob Steele, SERGEANT YORK ('41) with Gary Cooper, CALABOOSE ('42) with Jimmy Rogers, where he was cast as "Pidge," a nickname he was always known by, THE DALTONS RIDE AGAIN ('45), RED RIVER ('48) with John Wayne, a film that Beery claimed was his favorite all-time movie, DECISION AT SUNDOWN ('57) with Randolph Scott, INHERIT THE WIND ('60) with Spencer Tracy, and THE BEST LITTLE WHOREHOUSE IN TEXAS ('82) with Dolly Parton and Burt Reynolds.

Beery's guest television appearances were numerous and consisted of a variety of popular shows including "Gunsmoke," "Wagon Train," "Perry Mason," "Lassie," "The Virginian," "High Chaparral," "Alias Smith and Jones," "The Waltons," "The Love Boat," "Magnum P. I.," and "Murder, She Wrote." Beery probably gained his greatest measure of fame in television. His role as "Rocky," Jim Garner's dad in the long running hit series "The Rockford Files" earned him two Emmy nominations. Other television successes include hosting "The Noah Beery, Jr. Show" and roles in "Circus Boy," "Revenge of the Red Chief," "The Bastard," "The Great American Traffic Jam," "The Big Stuffed Dog," "Revenge of the Gray Gang," "Beyond Witch Mountain," "The Capture of Grizzly Adams," "Mysterious Two," and "The Quest." Noah also produced travel documentaries for television.

In 1940 Noah married Maxine Jones, the daughter of western star Buck Jones. The marriage produced three children—a son, Bucklind, and two daughters, Maxine and Melissa. Early on, the Beerys left the crowds and glitter of the Los Angeles area to make their home on a ranch in the Mojave Desert. Commenting on their choice of ranch living as opposed to city life, Noah remarked, "Heck, you just couldn't live there and believe all that stuff. You grow up and see all that and you know there has to be something better. I'll take living on my ranch any day."

Noah's son Bucklind, a third generation actor, commented, "We didn't even hang around Hollywood much. We always lived on a ranch and had lots of horses." Daughter Maxine added, "Daddy loved show business, but he never got caught up in it. He simply preferred to watch over his cattle and count his sheep."

After twenty-six years of marriage Beery and Maxine Jones divorced in 1966. Noah was married a second time in 1969 to new wife, Lisa. Lisa had two teenage children from a previous relationship.

Noah Beery, Jr. passed away on November 1, 1994, in Tehachapi, California. He lies at rest at Forest Lawn in the Hollywood Hills.

Some notes of possible interest:

• Noah's hobby was collecting Charles Russell paintings and sculptures. He was talented himself as a sculptor of western art objects.

• Beery's favorite western star was his father-in-law of many years, Buck Jones.

• Noah claimed his two most memorable movie-making experiences include working with Gary Cooper in the award-winning movie SERGEANT YORK and with Jimmy Stewart in THE SPIRIT OF SAINT LOUIS. Beery's most enjoyable cinema work was while teaming with Jimmy Rogers, son of Will Rogers, in a series of Hal Roach comedies. He and Jim remained friends for life.

• In 1990 Noah Beery received a Golden Boot Award.

• In the mid-'80s Beery suffered a stroke and remained in poor health until his death.

BOBBY BLAKE

Many of the juvenile players who appeared in western movies enjoyed but a brief moment in the sun, their fling with fame fast fleeting. They made only few appearances, then faded from the Hollywood scene, often never to be heard from again. Such was *not* the case with Bobby Blake. He rose from his roles as child actor and gained stature in films and television in his adult roles.

If you want to visit the place of Blake's birth, do not head for Brooklyn as offered by David Quinlan in *Quinlan's Illustrated Directory of Film Stars*, but travel to a place called Nutley, New Jersey. If one wishes to send a birthday card, September 18 was the day "Little Beaver" entered the world. However, if one desires to make a cake with the correct number of candles, there could be a problem. David Ragan in his *Who's Who in Hollywood* has Blake being born in 1933 (probably the correct year), but *Variety's Who's Who in Show Business* and David Dye in *Child and Youth Actors* both list 1934 as the correct year. In any event, the actor's given name was Michael James Vijencio Gubitosi, reason enough to become Bobby Blake.

According to published reports, Blake's childhood was not tantamount to life in "The Brady Bunch." He is alleged to have claimed he was an unplanned, unwanted child who was physically, emotionally, and sexually abused as a child. He has declined to state who the sexual abusers were, but relates that he was often beaten with a belt by his father and that his mother was sadistic and invented stories of his misbehavior to goad the father into unwarranted beatings. Blake once commented, "My father hated my success. He wanted to be there instead of me, and if not him, then the apple of his eye, my brother."

The family left New Jersey and headed for Hollywood. Legend has it members of the clan were at work as extras during the filming of one of the "Our Gang" series of shorts when one of the regulars couldn't remember his lines. Blake, the youngest of the three Gubitosi children, stepped in, and for the next several years played the role of "Mickey" in forty episodes.

It was in the mid-1940s Blake gained most of his recognition with fans of the westerns as he became "Little Beaver," the Indian boy sidekick of first Bill Elliott, and later Allan Lane, in the "Red Ryder" series. He appeared in 23 Ryder films where his speaking roles consisted of mainly, "You betchum, Red Ryder."

Blake claims his adolescent years were spent in turmoil. His schooling, largely at MGM, was a time when he says, "...nobody taught me anything. I couldn't read; I couldn't write." He further claims he was the victim of taunts and abuse by his peers. Late in life he discovered he was dyslexic.

One source writes Blake left his family at age 17 and joined the Army. However, he was still having roles in films up to 1953. He may have joined the Army at one time, because there is a three-year hiatus in his film credits during the mid-1950s. The same writer who has Blake entering the Army reports that after completion of his Army service he then resumed his acting career and entered psychotherapy. There is little doubt the actor's life was one of great turbulence, as he is alleged to have gone through problems with drugs, alcohol, and wild behavior.

Blake's sessions with his psychotherapist may not have had the desired effects. The actor is quoted as follows, "I asked him questions. He had no answers. It got worse and worse. One day I grabbed him by the collar and pulled him up over the desk, and I realized I was going to kill him. What had he ever done for me?" Inner conflicts continued to haunt Blake. In 1986 he had a starring role in the hit television series, "Hell Town," when he just walked off the set. He says, "I couldn't do it any more. I ran out of reasons for acting, reasons for living, and was only looking for the slightest reason to end it all."

Did the man possess talent? Unquestionably. His role in the film IN COLD BLOOD ('67) was among Hollywood's finest. His television series, "Baretta," was one of the more interesting and popular series, and Blake won an Emmy for outstanding lead actor in a drama series for "Baretta." He was nominated for an Emmy for his performance in the television film "Judgment Day: The John List Story" ('93). Blake had roles in a number of films with compelling performances such as TELL THEM WILLIE BOY IS HERE ('69), BLOOD FEUD ('83), and PORK CHOP HILL ('59). His western film credits (other than the Red Ryder series) include DAKOTA ('45) with John Wayne, HOME ON THE RANGE ('46) with Monte Hale, and THE LAST ROUNDUP ('47) with Gene Autry. He had some success behind the camera as well, producing television shows such as "Joe Dancer: The Big Trade," "Of Mice and Men," and "The Big Black Pill." He also did some of the directing in the "Baretta" series. Blake had many guest television appearances, among them "Adventures of Wild Bill Hickok," "The Cisco Kid," "Broken Arrow," "The Californians," "Zane Grey Theater," "Bat Masterson," "Wagon Train," "Laramie," and "Rawhide."

Blake's domestic life was no "Sea of Tranquility." In 1960 Blake married Sondra Kerr. The marriage endured until 1982 and produced a son and a daughter. Here too, there are reports of discord and violence. Friends report that on one occasion Blake threatened Kerr by putting a gun in her mouth. Kerr is alleged to have complained at the time the marriage was breaking up she was terrified of Blake, and he had forced her at gunpoint to tell their two children they had to live with him.

How do Blake's fellow actors perceive him? Pretty Peggy Stewart, who has known Blake since their days of working together in the "Red Ryder" westerns, said, "He's just as upright as he can be. A lovable, huggable kid. I adore him. I think he's generous to a fault." Others, however, had less than complimentary things to say about this accomplished actor, as he often had difficulty getting along with production people and cast members.

The "tangled web" of Blake's life continued as Blake became involved with Bonny Lee Bakley. According to media reports, Bakley was a scam artist, who was "star struck," and in efforts to further her station in life bedded down with a bevy of "names." Blake was one of the "names." As is wont to happen in these situations, Bakley found herself "heavy with child," and pointed the finger in Blake's direction. After consenting to a DNA test which identified him as the father, Blake married Bakley in November 2000. In May 2001 Bakley was shot to death while sitting in Blake's car after having dinner at an Italian restaurant. In the spring of 2002, Blake was charged by the Los Angeles County district attorney's office with first-degree murder for Bakley's death. As this book goes to press, Blake is out on bond awaiting trial in the homicide case. *Stay tuned . . . here comes another big Hollywood celebrity trial!*

SONNY BUPP

Sonny Bupp, born January 10, 1928, in New York City, was the youngest of the five Bupp children, four of whom made it as players in the world of the cinema. If your question is why he was billed as "Sonny," his given name at birth was Moyer MacClaren Bupp. In adult life, Sonny now answers to the nickname, "Mac."

Tom Bupp, Sonny's nephew and the son of Sonny's "Kid Kowboy" brother, Tommy Bupp, writes "Bupp's family was always on the move. They moved from New York to Florida to Washington and finally ended up in California. The family moved there because of his (Tommy's) father's asthma and the chance at a better job." Not long after the family arrived in California, Sonny's mother decided that Mr. Bupp's health was not a major concern and divorced him. Sonny writes, "My mother, a very aggressive woman, was bent on having all five of her children—three boys and two girls—in show business. With the exception of my oldest brother Paul, she made a real stab at having each of us become actors and actresses beginning with my oldest sister June, followed by my sister Ann, my brother Tom, and me, the youngest of the five."

Sonny's early years were spent involved in stage plays at the Pasadena Playhouse, a usual source used by studio talent scouts for discovering new faces. Sonny relates that he and sister Ann got many calls for roles as extras due to their activity at the Playhouse. "In fact," said Sonny, "I made *Variety* magazine as being the juvenile who made the most money as an extra in, I believe, 1935 or 1936." Sonny goes on, "My mother engaged an 'agent' for my brother and me, an ambitious fellow name Julian Olynick, who diligently pursued his purchased services (he received 10% of our salaries) by seeking out and finding parts for my brother Tommy and me."

On being a juvenile actor in films, Sonny says, "I never liked being a child actor in the movies, in fact, I dreaded seeing Mr. Olynick's car parked in front of our house knowing it meant going on another 'interview' (a visit to the casting director for a movie part). On the other hand, working on the stage was really fun. When you work in a stage play it's 'live,' playing to real people watching and listening to you from the audience. You and the other players start off by stumbling through your lines, working with a script until, after much rehearsing, all of you have your parts memorized, and are ready to 'let the show begin.' You develop a camaraderie among players, not like the movies, where you seldom develop any kind of a personal relationship with anyone, since it's a 'one shot' deal."

Sonny Bupp's movie career commenced in the early 1930s when he made appearances in shorts, including an "Our Gang" and some un-billed bit parts. Few western films are listed among his over 60 credits. He had roles in VALLEY OF THE GIANTS ('38) with Wayne Morris, THE RENEGADE TRAIL ('39) with William Boyd, THREE FACES WEST ('40) with John Wayne, BAD MEN OF MISSOURI ('41) with Dennis Morgan, WEST OF CIMARRON ('41) with the Three Mesquiteers trio of Bob Steele, Tom Tyler and Rufe Davis, and CODE OF THE OUTLAW ('41) with the same Mesquiteers.

Sonny made appearances in some of Hollywood's major films including roles in KID MILLIONS ('34), SAN FRANCISCO ('36), LOST HORIZON ('37), ANGELS WITH DIRTY FACES ('38), ABE LINCOLN IN ILLINOIS ('40), CITIZEN KANE ('41), SERGEANT YORK ('41), THE DEVIL AND DANIEL WEBSTER ('41) and TENNESSEE JOHNSON ('42). For his role in CITIZEN KANE, Sonny was picked from a group of boy actors by Orson Welles, the film's star and director. Welles felt Sonny so resembled him that he selected him without an audition. Sonny Bupp's last credited film was EYES OF THE UNDERWORLD ('43).

The Bupp brothers, Tommy and Sonny, made appearances together in a number of films including KID MILLIONS, SAN FRANCISCO, WOMAN WISE, LOVE IS ON THE AIR, SWING YOUR LADY, HUNTED MEN, WHEN TOMORROW COMES, NO PLACE TO GO, and QUEEN OF THE MOB.

Sonny had his problems. He writes: "Oddly enough, one of the biggest problems to me as a child was my hair. In the thirties boys did not wear their hair long! But, if you were a child actor, you never cut your hair. That is because if the part called for long hair, such as a period picture, you had long hair. If the part required short hair then they (the studio) cut it—simple. Simple except for the razzing and hazing I got every time I went back to regular school (when you worked in a movie, the studio provided the teachers.) The 'hair' problem, was a not-so-pleasant experience that most people could not know about."

The Bupp mother was another source of concern, as Sonny further states: "Of considerable dismay to me was the fact that, despite earning a considerable amount of money (I was paid $50.00 to $75.00 a day, when a regular man's salary was good at $25.00 a week) my mother never put aside a red cent of it for me. This was, incidentally, against the law, which required that 50% of a minor's earnings be put into a trust fund (the Coogan Law). My mother apparently felt that law didn't apply to her! I also got $18.00 a week unemployment compensation for any week I didn't work! I can still recall the looks on adult people's faces as I stood in line with them! (My mother made certain she picked me up from school and took me to get my check.) We never did find out for sure what she did with the money, although each in the family had their individual ideas and suspicions. Of significant note is the fact that, at the time, juvenile's incomes were not subject to federal income tax! (Adding, of course, to my unrealized net worth!) For many reasons I would never recommend that parents seek an acting career for their children. It's a very unnatural environment that, in many cases, can adversely affect a person's entire life. I was fortunate in not wanting or liking this type of lifestyle."

As his movie career came to an end, Sonny moved to northern California with his mother and stepfather. Sonny Bupp became an executive with the Ford Motor Company in Detroit, and later in Australia. Sonny married in 1972, and he and his wife were last reported living in Southfield, Michigan. The couple had no children.

TOMMY BUPP

Tommy Bupp was one of five children born to the Bupp household, four of whom had roles in films. Tommy was born on February 2, 1925, in Norfolk, Virginia. The Bupp family was constantly on the move from state to state, finally arriving in the Hollywood area in the late 1920s. It wasn't long before Tommy became the third member of the family to embark on a film career.

Young Tommy, with 100 film credits (many of them short subjects) during his early years, appeared in "Kid Kowboy" roles in thirteen oaters. His first credit was in HI-NEIGHBOR! ('34), an "Our Gang" short, and he ended his career in movies with NAVAL ACADEMY ('41). Tommy Bupp's western movie credits include THE MAN FROM HELL ('34) with Reb Russell, THE RAWHIDE TERROR ('34) with Art Mix and Edmund Cobb, ARIZONA BAD MAN ('35) and OUTLAW RULE ('35) both with Reb Russell, ROARIN' GUNS ('36) with Tim McCoy, SUTTER'S GOLD ('36) with Edward Arnold, ROARIN' LEAD ('36) a Three Mesquiteer western with Bob Livingston, Ray Corrigan and Max Terhune, ARIZONA DAYS and HITTIN' THE TRAIL ('37) both with Tex Ritter, CHEROKEE STRIP ('37) with Dick Foran, IT HAPPENED IN HOLLYWOOD ('37) with Richard Dix, and TEX RIDES WITH THE BOY SCOUTS ('38) with Tex Ritter. A note of possible interest: in THE CHEROKEE STRIP, Dick Foran sang a lullaby to Tommy, and the song, "My Little Buckaroo," became a hit.

Some of the more notable non-western films in which Tommy appeared are A GIRL OF THE LIMBERLOST ('34), KID MILLIONS ('34), BABES IN TOYLAND ('34), THE SCARLET LETTER ('34), LITTLE MEN ('35), THE HOOSIER SCHOOLMASTER ('35), AH, WILDERNESS ('35), LITTLE LORD FAUNTLEROY ('36), SAN FRANCISCO ('36), MARY OF SCOTLAND ('36), THE LONGEST NIGHT ('36), CAPTAIN COURAGEOUS ('37), LOVE IS ON THE AIR ('37), A SLIGHT CASE OF MURDER ('38), LITTLE ORPHAN ANNIE ('38), MR. SMITH GOES TO WASHINGTON ('39) and THE WAY OF ALL FLESH ('40).

Tommy had forays into avenues of the entertainment world other than his film roles. He provided the voice of some of the characters in animated cartoons, was a regular on the radio program

"Those O'Malleys," and performed on stage at the Pasadena Community Playhouse. After Hollywood, Tommy worked for a while as a gas station attendant. One day, on his lunch break, he met his future wife, Ruth, at a local diner. He became the stepfather of Russell Ice, Ruth's son. He and Ruth had four sons together—Tom, Jamie, Paul, and Billy.

Tommy's son Tom has the following to say about his dad: "Tommy was the first American child actor to travel to England to make a film, probably the British version of LOVE IS ON THE AIR, a Ronald Reagan film titled RADIO MURDER MYSTERY in 1937." Tom reports that on the return trip on the Queen Mary, Tommy and his mother became friends with a rich Kentucky horse breeder and they were invited to visit their ranch, where Tommy was presented with a racehorse as a gift. (No word as to what happened to the horse.) Tom also relates Tommy had hobbies like most American boys—stamp collecting, football, baseball, and marbles. Tom further reports that the union of Tommy and Ruth resulted in producing nine grandchildren: Jennifer, Sarah, Andy, Emilie, Juleah, Jessica, Erica, Traci, and Kristin. Tommy later worked for thirty years in the wholesale electrical business. Tommy's son, Tom, tells us his father passed away on December 24, 1983, in Santa Ana, California, at age 59, a victim of cancer.

MICHAEL CHAPIN

Michael Chapin was just one of three children in the Chapin family to have careers in the world of entertainment. His younger siblings, brother Billy and sister Lauren, both spent time before the camera. Michael's father, William Chapin, served as senior vice-president of Title Insurance and Trust Company of Los Angeles. His mother, Marguerite was, as Michael explained in a most positive way, a "movie mom," handling he and his siblings' requirements. His brother, Billy had screen roles in THE KID FROM LEFT FIELD, TOBOR THE GREAT, and NIGHT OF THE HUNTER. Sister Lauren was "Kitten" on television's "Father Knows Best."

Michael is able to claim he was the last of the cinema B-western stars, and it all happened before he was old enough to vote. Chapin was born in Hollywood on July 25, 1936, and made his screen debut at the age of eight with an un-credited role in THE FIGHTING SULLIVANS ('44), the story of the five Iowa brothers who lost their lives in the service during World War II. Over the course of a ten-year career, Chapin managed support roles with western stars commencing with his second film SONG OF ARIZONA ('44) with Roy Rogers. This was followed by appearances in UNDER CALIFORNIA STARS ('48) again with Roy Rogers, WELLS FARGO GUNMASTER ('51) with Allan "Rocky" Lane, WAGONS WEST ('52) with Rod Cameron, and SPRINGFIELD RIFLE ('52) with Gary Cooper.

In the late '40s, Republic Studios was conducting a search for a youthful twosome to star in westerns as sort of a junior version of Roy Rogers and Dale Evans. Picked for the roles were Chapin and Eileen Janssen. The duo, billed as "The Rough Ridin' Kids," appeared together in a series of four oaters: BUCKAROO SHERIFF OF TEXAS ('51), THE DAKOTA KID ('51), ARIZONA MANHUNT ('51) and WILD HORSE AMBUSH ('52), after which it was pretty much "so long" to Republic's B-westerns.

Among Michael's other film credits are SONG OF THE SOUTH ('45) where only his laughing voice was heard, THE CORN IS GREEN ('45) with Bette Davis, NIGHTWIND ('46) with Charles Russell and Gary Gray, IT'S A WONDERFUL LIFE ('46) with Jimmy Stewart, NIGHT EDITOR ('46) with William Gargan, HEAVEN ONLY KNOWS ('46) with Robert Cummings, BACKLASH ('47) with Jean Rogers and Gary Gray, THE BOY WITH GREEN HAIR ('48) with Dean Stockwell, CALL NORTHSIDE 777 ('48) with Jimmy Stewart, STRANGE BARGAIN ('49) with Jeffrey Lynn, SUMMER STOCK ('49) with Judy Garland, Gene Kelly and Teddy Infuhr, PRIDE OF THE BLUEGRASS ('53) with Arthur Shields and Vera Miles, and NIGHT OF THE HUNTER ('54) with Robert Mitchum, Shelly Winters, Lillian Gish, and Michael's brother, Billy Chapin.

Motion pictures were not the only avenues in the world of entertainment for Michael. In 1946 he was on stage at the Phoenix-Westwood Theatre with Albert Dekker in "Father Was President." By age 13, he had appeared on radio in "Adventure Playhouse," "Anne and Mac Show," "Arch Obler Comedy Theater," "Jack Benny Show," "Blondie," "Burns and Allen," "Dr. Christian," "Command Performance," "Dennis Day Show," "Ford Theatre," "Family Theatre," "Hollywood Star Theatre," "Straight Arrow," "Phil Harris and Alice Faye Show," "Voice of the Army," and as an ongoing cast member of "One Man's Family."

On live television, he was in the series "Who's News" in 1949-'50 and in 1954 was with Margaret O'Brien on "Lux Video Theatre." Michael's television guest appearances include "The Lone Ranger" ('49).

Michael's education was in private schools, St. John's Military Academy and Loyola High School in Los Angeles. He is a graduate of the prestigious Massachusetts Institute of Technology in Cambridge, Massachusetts, with a degree in math. Chapin served in the U.S. Army as a member of the 11th Airborne as a paratrooper. He was stationed in Europe where he says he saw most of Europe and North Africa. While in the service, he learned German and frequented many museums, art galleries and operas.

Michael married his wife Carolyn, a former United Airlines flight attendant, on August 26, 1966. The couple have three children—Douglas, a film editor at Warner Brothers; Christopher, a loan officer; and Carin, the Deputy Director of Public Relations at Pepperdine University. Michael and Carolyn have six grandchildren and two great-grandchildren.

Michael is the owner and headmaster of a private Montessori School in Los Angeles and works as a computer software architect. His hobbies are backpacking, traveling, and flying Cessna and ultra-light planes. He is also an instructor of flying for these crafts.

Asked his favorite roles, he listed the "wanna-be boyfriend" of Margaret O'Brien in Lux Theatre's, "The Way We Were," his cameo role in NIGHT OF THE HUNTER, and his role as "Red" in BUCKAROO SHERIFF OF TEXAS. He says his favorite performer is actress Rosalind Russell. His close friends in the movie industry include Gary Gray, Gigi Perreau, and Tommy Ivo.

As of August 2002, the Chapins are traveling full time in their motor home criss-crossing all of North America. Michael Chapin personifies all that is good about the world of entertainment and our country.

BOBBY CLARK

Bobby Clark, whose real surname was Clack, was born in the small Oklahoma town of Spiro, on January 3, most probably in 1926. He received his early schooling in nearby Talihina. His father, Arnold Clack, a rancher and gas station owner, noticed early on that his son had a talent and interest in performing with a rope. The two started attending rodeos with Bobby first performing his roping expertise at the age of six in Springfield, Missouri. Over the next few years Bobby continued to develop his talent as a roper as well as becoming adept at performing with a rifle and a six-shooter.

The Fourth of July, 1938, was the day Hollywood's doors opened up for Bobby Clark. It was on that date, while performing at a rodeo in Sulphur, Oklahoma, that he was noticed by a Monogram talent scout and signed. He made his debut supporting Jack Randall in TRIGGER SMITH ('39). Later that year it is reported thirteen-year-old Clark, with his horse "Chief," appeared at a rodeo in Madison Square Garden and won the world champion trick roping title. Returning to Hollywood, he appeared as the juvenile co-star to Bill Elliott in the serial OVERLAND WITH KIT CARSON ('39).

In 1940 Bobby was given star status and billed as "13-year-old world's champion junior cowboy" in PDC's western feature THE SAGEBRUSH FAMILY TRAILS WEST. Clark then returned home to finish his schooling in Poteau, Oklahoma. He moved on to Fort Smith, Arkansas, where he continued performing on the rodeo circuit. The next thing we heard about Clark is that he reportedly served in the U.S. Army during World War II, including an 18-month hitch in the Philippines.

He married Ruth Lee, an Idaho girl, in 1946. It could not be determined whether Bobby Clark ever fathered children.

He is said to have toured with Allan Lane in 1947. Back in Hollywood after a hiatus of several years, Bobby supported Sunset Carson in RIO GRANDE ('49) and had a small role in the cliffhanger MAN WITH THE STEEL WHIP ('54). Among his western film appearances are credited roles in the following Gene Autry oaters, RIM OF THE CANYON ('49), SONS OF NEW MEXICO ('50), BEYOND THE PURPLE HILLS ('50), SILVER CANYON ('51), THE OLD WEST ('52), and BARBED WIRE ('62). In addition to his film career, rodeo performances, and personal appearance tours, Bobby Clark was a frequent television guest.

Of possible interest, Clark's father had a brief Hollywood fling as he appeared in a non-speaking heavy role with Tim McCoy in TEXAS RENEGADES ('40). He later worked as a used car salesman in Phoenix, Arizona.

Bobby Clark is said to have "ridden off into the sunset" sometime in 1986.

BILL CODY, JR.

Imagine, if you will, growing up as the son of one of Hollywood's B-western cowboy heroes. Imagine further, that at an early age you got to play "Kid Cowboy" sidekick roles—not only with your famous father, but also with the likes of Johnny Mack Brown and Tom Keene. Such was the boyhood of Bill Cody, Jr.

Long lost in the mysteries of whatever happened to some of the western players who made life so pleasurable for many, we can (thanks to the man I consider the best of the Hollywood western player researchers, Luther Hathcock of Hickory, North Carolina) learn details of the life and times of Bill Cody, Jr. Due to Luther's painstaking research and diligence—in not only locating this former juvenile star, but also by conducting personal interviews with Cody—the following story emerges:

William Joseph Cody, Jr. was born on April 18, 1925, at a hospital in Hollywood. Young Cody's father was born in Winnipeg, Canada, and attended college in the United States at Saint John's University in Minnesota. Unlikely as it seems, the western star's true name was William Cody, thus debunking a popular legend that the cinema cowboy took the name of the original "Buffalo Bill."

The senior Cody, born on January 5, 1891, went to work as a stuntman at the old Biograph Studios in New York around 1912. He arrived in Hollywood in 1920 where he first worked in melodramas. It wasn't until 1925, the year of young Bill's birth, that Bill Cody, Sr. first saddled up his horse "Chico" and became one of Hollywood's western stars. Bill Junior's mother was an English lady, Victoria Kench. The Codys' marriage was, by all accounts, an enduring one. There was also a second son, Hank, born into the Cody clan.

Many of the comments made by the former child star to Luther will be of interest to western fans. Bill related that Andy Shuford was the original juvenile sidekick to his father and appeared in eight westerns with the senior Cody. When Shuford grew too mature for the role, the father decided it was time to bring Junior into the act. They teamed in several westerns in the early 1930s, including such oaters as FRONTIER DAYS ('34), BORDER GUNS ('34), THE VANISHING RIDER ('35), THE RECKLESS BUCKAROO ('35), and OUTLAWS OF THE RANGE ('36).

Can the reader remember those days in the '30s when the circus came to town and one of Hollywood's cowboys was a star attraction? Bill Cody was one of those cowboys, and often he was accompanied by Bill, Jr., much to the delight of young fans.

Bill related that one of the things he enjoyed as a youth was listening to his father's friend, Al Jennings, tell stories of his train robbing days when Jennings was a real wild west outlaw. "I knew all those guys," Bill related to Hathcock, "Franklyn Farnum, Bill Desmond, Art Mix, Bud Osborne, Tom Keene, Jack Perrin, Yak Canutt, and George O'Brien—they were all friends of my father's."

In addition to roles in his father's westerns, Bill also played the part of the young cowboy with other western heroes. He supported Tom Keene in ROMANCE OF THE ROCKIES ('37), Johnny Mack Brown and Bob Baker in DESPERATE TRAILS ('39), Charles Starrett in TWO-FISTED RANGERS ('40), Johnny Mack Brown in BAD MAN FROM RED BUTTE ('40) and Bill "Cowboy Rambler" Boyd in RAIDERS OF THE WEST ('42). Of Brown, Bill said, "A true southern gentleman who always had time for me. He was a very important person in my young life."

There were film roles other than B-westerns in Bill's life. One of the more memorable is his portrayal of Nelson Eddy as a young boy in GIRL OF THE GOLDEN WEST ('38). His two favorite roles were both in serials—with Johnny Mack Brown in THE OREGON TRAIL ('39), and with Jackie Cooper and Junior Coghlan in SCOUTS TO THE RESCUE ('39). Bill had one other serial to his credit, a small part in SKY RAIDERS ('41). He also had an un-credited part in the mega-film DESTRY RIDES AGAIN ('39) that starred Jimmy Stewart and Marlene Dietrich.

The year 1941 proved to be the final year of Bill Cody, Jr.'s Hollywood career. The young Cody quit school and enlisted in the U.S. Navy, serving in the South Pacific. His brother Hank also saw combat during the war. Returning home after the war, Bill was offered contracts to return to acting, but as he related to Hathcock, "After the war, my desire to go back to the studio was gone, so I left the business. This hurt my father, but he accepted it as my choice." Bill returned to Hollywood High School after the war and graduated.

On April 22, 1948, Bill married his long time sweetheart, "Liz" McGregor, a marriage that lasted until her death. This union produced a son who became a carpenter. The son, in return, married, and little Canyon Cody became Bill's pride and joy as his only grandchild. Following his film career, Bill Cody, Jr. worked for many years as an executive with a Los Angeles credit collection firm.

Bill's wife passed away in 1988 of cancer. Sadly, Bill Cody, Jr. died at age 64 in his Studio City, California, apartment on August 11, 1989, a suicide victim. In a note to his family, he wrote how hard the past 16 months had been without his beloved wife, and that he missed her so much he no longer cared to go on living without her. His son, grandson, and brother were his survivors. Cody is buried beside his wife in Forest Lawn Cemetery.

JUNIOR COGHLAN

Frank Coghlan, Jr., known best to film fans as simply Junior Coghlan, has film credits commencing from 1920. Junior was born in New Haven, Connecticut, on May 16, 1917. Shortly after his birth, Coghlan's father, a railroad clerk and a part time professional boxer, moved the family to California where Junior, as well as his father and mother, all worked as extras in silent films.

Junior's first film role occurred when he was three years of age with an un-credited role in a film titled, MID-CHANNEL ('20). Hundreds of movies would follow during a Hollywood tenure of several decades, interrupted by years of service to his country. In spite of the large number of his film appearances, Junior's western credits are not numerous. In an interview with the British western journal, *Wrangler's Roost*, Junior said his first western film appearance was a 1920 western with Tom Santschi called THE SIN BUSTER but says that no record of a film by that title can now be verified. Among his credited western films as a juvenile actor are the following: In 1926 Junior had roles supporting H.B. Warner in WHISPERING SMITH, and was with William Boyd and Jack Hoxie in THE LAST FRONTIER. RIVER'S END with Charles Bickford in 1930, and DRUM TAPS with Ken Maynard in 1933. This marked the end for Junior as a western kid actor. During these years, Junior did make appearances in two non-westerns with soon-to-be cinema cowboy William Boyd in HER MAN O' WAR ('26) and THE YANKEE CLIPPER ('27).

37

As a youngster, Junior had the same interest that many youngsters enjoyed—he was an avid stamp collector. At La Conte Junior High School, he was president of his class in 1931 and participated in football and track. In 1927 he had the role of the batboy in the film about the great New York Yankee baseball team of that year, SLIDE, KELLY, SLIDE. In preparation for his role, Junior lived every boy's dream as he got to spend six weeks with the team and to meet Babe Ruth and Lou Gehrig.

The first of Junior's "talkies" was his western with Charles Bickford, RIVER'S END ('30). In RACETRACK (32) with Leo Carrillo, Junior, with no stuntman involved, played a jockey and did his own riding in the big race. Coghlan had three serials among his many credits. In his first serial he had one of the leads in the role of "Uncas" when he joined up with Harry Carey in THE LAST OF THE MOHICANS ('32). During filming, Junior was a student at Fairfax High School, a school from which he would graduate in 1934. He was a member of the lightweight football team and the track squad. The late George Katchmer, one of Western films better historians, wrote in an issue of *Classic Images* as follows:

> It was in track, however, that Junior excelled in the hurdles. He led the hurdlers for two years. The city meet was approaching, and he was in the process of filming the serial THE LAST OF THE MOHICANS. To maintain his timing, he took a set of hurdles on location and practiced daily. On the day of the city meet director Ford Beebe had the studio limousine escort Junior to the track which waited to escort him back to the set. The hitch here was that he was due back on the set as soon as he finished his event. So to the amazement and amusement of trackmen and crowd, Junior ran the race complete with Mohican war paint, scalp lock, and all. He came in second, and the event is still the talk at school reunions.

Katchmer continues:

> The fact that the filming of THE LAST OF THE MOHICANS took ten weeks to complete caused him some trouble with an algebra teacher who would not accept his studio grades. This caused him to go an extra semester and held up his graduation until the summer session was over. He immediately enrolled at U.C.L.A. He did not graduate from that institution as he had many interruptions and continued his acting.

Junior's next serial was SCOUTS TO THE RESCUE ('39) with Jackie Cooper, Bill Cody, Jr., and Vondell Darr. Part of the serial was filmed in the Dardanelle Mountains of California, and in one scene Cooper, Darr and Coghlan were in a canoe that overturned in the rapids. Cooper made it safely to shore, but Darr was in trouble, and the young lady was saved by Junior. Coghlan's final serial, and the screen role for which he is best remembered by fans, was as Billy Batson in AD-VENTURES OF CAPTAIN MARVEL ('41) with cowboy star Tom Tyler as the lead.

Junior, as is the case with most young men, had his share of girlfriends and romantic flings. His first teenage romance was with Mitzi Green. He also dated Anne Shirley, Juanita Quigley's older sister Rita and Margie Keeler, the younger sister of Ruby Keeler. His most serious Hollywood romance was with Noel Neill, whom he dated for two years. The two met while both were appearing in the Henry Aldrich series with Jimmy Lydon.

Up until the World War II years, Coghlan had a myriad of roles in a number of pictures, including PENROD AND SAM ('31) with Zasu Pitts, CHARLIE CHAN AT THE RACE TRACK ('36) with Warner Oland, ANGELS WITH DIRTY FACES ('38) with Jimmy Cagney, Pat O'Brien, and Humphrey Bogart, DUST BE MY DESTINY ('39) with John Garfield, THE FIGHTING 69TH ('40) with Cagney and O'Brien again, KNUTE ROCKNE ALL AMERICAN ('40) again with O'Brien, and Ronald Reagan, HENRY ALDRICH FOR PRESIDENT ('41) with Jimmy Lydon, THE MAN WHO CAME TO DINNER ('42) with Monte Woolly and Bette Davis, and THE COURT-SHIP OF ANDY HARDY ('42) with Mickey Rooney.

In GONE WITH THE WIND ('39) readers may recall the furor that was raised when Clark Gable uttered the words, "Frankly my dear, I don't give a damn." Junior had a bit part in the film playing a Confederate soldier who was wounded. As he is picked up by a fellow soldier, he said, "Put me down, damn ya, I can walk." It was cut from the film due to the fuss over Gable's "damn." Times have changed.

In 1942, with World War II raging, Junior enlisted in the Navy's flight program. He enjoyed life as a naval aviator and loved flying. At the war's end he made the difficult choice of a naval career over returning to Hollywood. He spent 23 years in active duty and accumulated 4,500 hours of flight time. Among his post war assignments were tours of duty at the Pentagon and as public affairs officer. He worked closely with Hollywood on films that had navy themes such as THE CAINE MUTINY, THE BRIDGES AT TOKO-RI, MR. ROBERTS, THE WACKIEST SHIP IN THE NAVY, ALL HANDS ON DECK, and P.T. 109, as he headed the motion picture section of the Navy Office of Information. Junior retired from the Navy on June 30, 1965, with the rank of lieutenant commander.

Following his navy career Junior returned to Hollywood and had lesser roles in several films. His last picture was supporting John Wayne in IN HARM'S WAY ('65), after which he retired. Junior did a few guest spots on television, and for several years he served as pitchman for several firms including Curtis Mathis.

In 1945 at the Pensacola, Florida, Naval Air Base, Coghlan served as best man at the wedding of his roommate. The bride's maid of honor was Betty Corrigan of St. Louis, Missouri. It was a case of love at first sight, and three months later Betty Corrigan became Mrs. Frank Coghlan. The marriage was a happy one that lasted for 28 years until Betty passed away in her sleep from a massive stroke. The couple was blessed with five children.

Eight months after Betty's death, a friend called Junior to ask if he was ready to resume his social life. When Junior answered in the affirmative, the friend set up a dinner date and a bridge game with his recently-divorced sister-in-law. The couple started dating, and eight months later Frank married Letha. Letha had three sons from her prior marriage. Junior's five children from his marriage to Betty and Letha's three sons got along well enough so that there were a total of ten grandchildren.

Junior's five children from his marriage to Betty have all had positive lives. All did some limited film work but did not continue as actors. Mike, the oldest son, worked as a grip on the STAR TREK series. Son Pat worked as a high school teacher and coached football. He appeared in several episodes of the "Dennis The Menace" television series. Daughter Libbey has a masters' degree in dance from U.C.L.A. and is a choreographer. Cathy became a talented gymnast and later taught the sport. Youngest daughter Judy was associated with an automobile dealership.

Into their retirement years, Junior and Letha traveled extensively with two trips to Europe, several trips to different parts of Mexico, visited islands in the Caribbean, and cruised to Alaska. They were often on the golf course, and they enjoyed photography. Junior also became an author, as he penned his autobiography, *They Still Call Me Junior*. Sadly, wife Letha passed away in December 2001. At last reports, Junior was residing with a daughter.

TOMMY COOK

Tommy Cook received his "baptism of fire" as a "Kid Kowboy" when he played "Little Beaver" in the serial ADVENTURES OF RED RYDER ('40) with Don "Red" Barry in the title role. The following year he was back in the second of his two serial roles when he played a wild boy in JUNGLE GIRL ('41) starring Frances Gifford as "Nyoka, Queen of the Jungle."

Tommy Cook was born on July 5, 1930, in Duluth, Minnesota. He had three juvenile western roles: he appeared in WANDERER OF THE WASTELAND (45) with James Warren, in THE GAY SENORITA ('45) with Jinx Falkenberg and Jim Bannon, and in SONG OF ARIZONA ('46) with Roy Rogers.

As an adult, Cook continued playing western roles in DAUGHTER OF THE WEST ('49) with Phillip Reed, ROSE OF CIMARRON ('52) with Jack Beutel and Bob Steele, BATTLE OF APACHE PASS ('52) with John Lund and Jeff Chandler, THUNDER PASS ('54) with Dane Clark, CANYON CROSSROADS ('55) with Richard Basehart, MOHAWK ('56) with Scott Brady, and NIGHT PASSAGE ('57) with Jimmy Stewart and Audie Murphy.

Among Cook's non-western films of note are THE TUTTLES OF TAHITI ('42) with Charles Laughton and Jon Hall, HI, BUDDY ('43) with Dick Foran, STRANGE HOLIDAY ('46) with Claude Rains, GALLANT JOURNEY ('46) with Glenn Ford, TARZAN AND THE LEOPARD WOMAN ('46) with Johnny Weissmuller, PANIC IN THE STREETS ('50) with Richard Widmark, AN AMERICAN GUERRILLA IN THE PHILIPPINES ('50) with Tyrone Power, STALAG 17 ('53) with William Holden, and SEND ME NO FLOWERS ('64) with Rock Hudson and Doris Day. He also had the distinction of appearing in Audie Murphy's first film, BAD BOY ('49), along with Lloyd Nolan. Cook's final film credit was THE THING WITH TWO HEADS ('72) with Ray Milland and football great "Rosie" Grier. Tommy is also credited with being both the writer and producer of the Henry Fonda film ROLLERCOASTER ('77).

During the decade 1967-77, Tommy did voice work in several television cartoon shows, among them "The Superman/Aquaman Hour of Adventure," "Funky Phantom," "Jeannie," "Cop on the Beat," "Jabberjaw," and "Fred Flintstone and Friends." Among his television guest appearances were roles on "Adventures of Wild Bill Hickok," "The Life and Legend of Wyatt Earp," "Richard

Diamond, Private Detective," "Perry Mason," "Zane Grey Theater," "Man Without a Gun," "The Deputy," "The Lawless Years," "The Rifleman," and "CHiPs."

A comprehensive article by Tom Weaver in *Classic Images* provides some insight into the versatile and talented life of Tommy Cook:

> The Cook family's migration from Minnesota to Hollywood was not caused by Tommy's discovery by a movie agent, or even by thoughts of an acting career, but due to a medical necessity. Tommy's father, an obviously brilliant man, who graduated from Harvard University in three years (rather than the usual four) was stricken with Bright's disease and remained a lifelong invalid. The doctors advised the senior Cook to seek a warmer climate, and the family made the trek westward.

> While Tommy's father was forced to travel by train due to his health, the rest of the family—Tommy, his sister, their mother, and their maternal grandmother—hired a man to drive them west. The trip was not without problems. In Van Horn, Texas, the driver of the Cooks' car fell asleep and an oncoming vehicle, whose driver was drunk, met their car head on. The accident resulted in injuries to all of the occupants, but the most serious of the injuries were Tommy's. He suffered severe facial lacerations requiring surgery.

> After arriving in California, Tommy's mother, recognizing his flair for performing, enrolled her son in the Ben Bard Playhouse and later at the famed Pasadena Playhouse, where he had roles in several plays. Responding to an offer for free auditions at NBC, Tommy was offered some roles in radio before there were any thoughts of becoming "Little Beaver."

Cook recalled, among his first film roles, an RKO short with Edgar Kennedy, MUTINY IN THE COUNTY, and THE GREENIE, at MGM. He later auditioned for, and was selected as Little Beaver in the "Red Ryder" serial.

Some points of interest were gleaned over the years from a myriad of sources relating to Tommy Cook:

• His education was in the public schools where his parents wanted him to have a more "social democratic" education than they felt Hollywood professional schools could offer. Tommy was offered a scholarship at the University of Southern California, but elected to attend U.C.L.A. His education was interrupted after a year when he became a U.S. Marine and served in the Philippines.

• Cook was one of southern California's leading junior tennis players, and later became one of the area's leading tennis professional teachers with many of Hollywood's elite as his students. Numbered among his students were Dean Martin, Jr., Janet Leigh, Desi Arnaz, Jr., Jim Bannon, and Steven Spielberg. Tommy has promoted several celebrity tennis, golf, and concert tournaments, and has made appearances in many venues.

• Of the many different entertainment media in which Tommy performed, his favorite was radio, not only for his roles as Junior Riley in "The Life of Riley," as Alexander Bumstead in "Blondie," or "Little Beaver" in radio's "Red Ryder," but also because of the actors he worked with on his radio shows.

Not only as a "Kid Kowboy," but also in a number of endeavors in his professional life, Tommy ranks among the successful. But, it was during a conversation with Tommy at the 2002 Memphis Film Festival that most impressed the author and defined Tommy Cook as a human being. Opening his wallet, Tommy brought out dozens of photos of children. "This is my son Michael," he said with obvious pride as he pointed to several pictures of a good-looking teenager. "He lives with me." Next were several photos of a pretty young girl. "This is Sara Jane, my adopted daughter. I was in Ecuador with Pancho Segura on a tennis tour when I met this orphan. I wanted a better life for her. It took a lot of legal work, but she now lives with me." Then came more pictures of another beautiful young lady. "This is Claire. I'm not her biological father, but we spend a lot of time together." My interest piqued, I asked more about Claire. Tommy related that his wife (now ex-wife) engaged in a liaison with her attorney employer, which resulted in Claire entering the world. Tommy went on to express his love for Claire and to say they did many things together, that he provided her with health insurance and other support, and continued by saying, "She tells everyone, even her biological father, Tommy is my 'real' dad."

To paraphrase a line from Rudyard Kipling's Gunga Din: You're a bigger man than I am, Tommy Cook.

JOHNNY CRAWFORD

Johnny Crawford is best remembered by western fans for his role as Mark McCain, the son of Chuck Connors, in the television series "The Rifleman."

Johnny was born in Los Angeles on March 26, 1946. His entry into the world of entertainment was as a "Mousketeer" in the popular television show "The Mickey Mouse Club" ('55). His brother Bobby was also a member of the group. Bobby later co-starred on television's "Laramie" with Robert Fuller and John Smith.

Johnny Crawford's venture into the "big screen" world commenced with a starring role in COURAGE OF BLACK BEAUTY ('57). His one juvenile role as a "Kid Kowboy" was in INDIAN PAINT ('63) with Jay Silverheels.

As an adult Crawford had support roles in two quality westerns with distinguished stars, as he appeared in EL DORADO ('67) with John Wayne, and in THE SHOOTIST ('76), Wayne's final film that also had Lauren Bacall and Jimmy Stewart as cast members.

Among Johnny's non-western films, he had a co-starring role with Tommy Kirk in VILLAGE OF THE GIANTS ('65), a lead role in THE NAKED APE ('73), and a chance to display his singing voice in his final credited movie, THE THIRTEENTH FLOOR ('99), for which he also served as historic music consultant and music director.

Crawford had significant parts in several television films including "The Gambler: The Adventure Continues" ('83) with Kenny Rogers, "All American Cowboy" ('85), "Adventures of William Tell" ('86), "The Gambler Returns: The Luck of the Draw" ('91), and "Child Stars: Their Story" ('00) in which he plays himself. Counted among his numerous television guest spots are stints on "The Lone Ranger," "Have Gun Will Travel," "Zane Grey Theater," "Trackdown," "The Restless Gun," "Rawhide," "Lancer," "The Big Valley," "Murder, She Wrote," and "Paradise."

Crawford's acting career has to be termed a success. He was nominated for an Emmy for his role in "The Rifleman," but working before the camera was not his true love. Music and singing were highlights in Johnny's life. In auditioning for a role as a "Mouseketeer" it was his imitation of Johnny Ray—a popular vocalist of the time, made famous by his rendition of the song "Cry"— that got Crawford his entry into "The Mickey Mouse Club."

Johnny's family background was heavy with theatrical and music heritage. His father was a film editor for Columbia Pictures, and Johnny says that whenever the studio needed little kids for a scene in a film under production he, or his brother or sister, would be put in as an extra. Johnny's mother, an actress and pianist, was for a time under contract to Warner Bros. His maternal grandmother, along with her sister, was in vaudeville and performed on the Keith Orpheum circuit. She was also a violinist. His maternal grandfather, also a violinist, served as concertmaster of the New York, Minneapolis, and Los Angeles Philharmonic Orchestras. Crawford's paternal grandmother was a pianist who performed in Chicago. His paternal grandfather was the head of a highly successful music publishing business and was later hired as the head of the songwriting department at Warner Brothers.

During his years on "The Rifleman," Johnny found the time to enhance his other interests. He recorded some albums and singles for Del-Fi, and some of his songs, such as "Cindy's Birthday," "Rumors," and "Your Nose is Gonna Grow," made national top-ten lists. In addition, he worked diligently on his riding and roping skills to the point that after high school he spent time competing on the American Junior Rodeo Association Circuit in Oklahoma, Texas, Colorado, and New Mexico in events such as steer wrestling, calf roping, and bareback bronc riding.

Johnny graduated from Hollywood High School in 1964. In the mid-'60s, Johnny was drafted and served a hitch in the Army. During this period, one writer, David Ragan, has Crawford working as a longshoreman.

Following his Army discharge, Johnny returned to do some movie and television work, but into the '80s his main focus was on his music career—he loved playing and singing folk songs. By the late '80s he was the vocalist for the Vince Giordano Nighthawk Orchestra. One of Johnny's highlights was playing at George Bush's inaugural ball in 1989. Into the '90s, he formed his own dance band, The Johnny Crawford Dance Orchestra, a highly popular band that features the music of the swing era of the 1920s, '30s, and early '40s.

Some notes, comments, and favorite moments in the life of Johnny Crawford:

• "I just love playing baseball."

• "I used to love The Cisco Kid and Hopalong Cassidy."

- "Gary Cooper was definitely one of my heroes."

- "Chuck had the whole team sign my baseball. Gus Bell gave me his bat, and we ate at Stan Musial's restaurant." (Commenting after he and Chuck Connors, while on a public relations tour in St. Louis, attended a Cardinal-Cubs game together at Sportsman's Park. Chuck Connors was a professional baseball and basketball player before becoming "The Rifleman.")

- "I really love being a band leader and enjoy it more than any other job I've ever had."

In 1990 Johnny and his high school sweetheart met again after a twenty-seven year separation. In 1995 he and Charlotte married in a ceremony held at Will Rogers State Park. It was Johnny's first venture into wedlock. Today the couple reside in a home in the Hollywood Hills with their "family" of rescued animals.

FRANKIE DARRO

Sitting in the theatre on a Saturday afternoon, watching the coming attractions and discovering that the next week's show was a Frankie Darro and Tom Tyler oater, was *almost* as good as being told that next week's treat was a Bob Steele thriller. Frankie Darro was certainly one of the more entertaining of the "Kid Kowboys."

Born on December 22, 1917, as Frank Johnson, in Chicago, Illinois, Frankie was the son of parents who were both circus performers and aerialists with Sells Brothers' Circus. The family later moved to California where Frankie's father was employed as a Hollywood stuntman. Frankie made his film debut at the age of six with a part in the 1924 Wallace Beery motion picture, JUDGMENT OF THE STORM. During several of Frankie's early film appearances he was billed as Frankie Darrow.

Over the years Frankie appeared in westerns with several of Hollywood's cowboy stars, including Harry Carey, Gene Autry, and Bill Elliott, but it was his roles as the juvenile sidekick of Tom Tyler that were by far the best. In addition to his many western features, Darro was a popular regular in what we used to refer to as "the chapters" with strong roles in the following serials: THE LIGHTNING WARRIOR ('31) with Rin Tin Tin, THE VANISHING LEGION ('31) with Harry Carey, THE DEVIL HORSE ('32) again with Carey and Rex, "King of the Wild Horses," THE WOLF DOG ('33) again with Rin Tin Tin, BURN 'EM UP BARNES ('34) with Jack Mulhall, THE PHANTOM EMPIRE ('35) with Gene Autry, THE GREAT ADVENTURES OF WILD BILL HICKOK ('38) with Bill Elliott, and JUNIOR G-MEN OF THE AIR ('42) with Billy Halop of "Dead End Kids" fame as the lead character.

Frankie's movie career was not limited to westerns and serials. He had roles in a number of other films, many of them "A" features such as THREE ON A MATCH ('32), TUGBOAT ANNIE ('33), WILD BOYS OF THE ROAD ('33), a film that many critics rated as Frankie's best performance, and LITTLE MEN ('35). Because of his small stature, in several films Frankie played the role of a jockey. He was rated as a very good rider.

During World War II, Frankie served in the U.S. Navy. Following the end of the war, Frankie returned to Hollywood and appeared in numerous films, including some westerns. Among his post war movies are FIGHTING FOOLS ('49) with Leo Gorcey and Huntz Hall, SONS OF NEW MEXICO ('49) with Gene Autry, WYOMING MAIL ('50) with Stephen McNally, ACROSS THE WIDE MISSOURI ('51) with Clark Gable, THE LAWLESS RIDER ('54) where he shared top billing with Douglas Dumbrille, and THE CARPETBAGGERS ('64) with Carroll Baker and George Peppard. Darro's final film credit was FUGITIVE LOVERS ('75) where he portrayed the town drunk.

Frankie—as did many of the screen actors of those days—made appearances on a variety of television programs. He gained a certain measure of fame by regularly portraying a little old lady on Red Skelton's comedy show. (There is nothing to indicate Darro dressed in "drag" at times other than on Skelton's show.) Frankie's last known television appearance was in the role of a studio guard in "Girl on the Late, Late Show" in 1974.

Darro's personal life was not without intrigue. Frankie's first trip on the sea of matrimony was to actress/dancer, Aloha Wray. Several sources have reported that Wray committed suicide while married to Frankie, but this is not true. A recently-discovered obituary on Wray confirmed that she had, in fact, committed suicide in her Hollywood apartment on April 28, 1968, at age forty, but that she had much earlier said "aloha" to Frankie, and her body was discovered by her estranged husband, Art Jones, a Hollywood laborer. She was survived by her mother.

Several of the Los Angeles newspapers dated July 24, 1951, make reference to the second Mrs. Darro, Betty Marie Darro, filing for divorce. The articles make reference to the fact Darro's first wife was Aloha Wray. Los Angeles newspapers, reporting further on the divorce hearing in an article dated November 25, 1951, cite the following:

> The couple was married on March 16, 1943. The second Mrs. Darro was given custody of the couple's daughter, Darlene, age five. Mrs. Darro alleged, as grounds for the divorce, that Frankie drank to excess, struck her while he was intoxicated, and that he had bought her presents—a washing machine, a toaster, a sewing machine, and a wrist watch—but that they were all repossessed within six months because Frankie failed to make any payments. Darro was ordered by the court to make child support payments of $75 a month and to pay Mrs. Darro $1 a month in token alimony.

The Darros next made headlines on September 30, 1954, when the ex-Mrs. Darro had Frankie arrested for failure to pay child support, past due in the amount of $1,570. Frankie was released from jail on bail of $500 posted by a friend. Frankie's comment when arrested was, "She can't get blood out of a rock."

According to the *Los Angeles Times* of October 23, 1957, Frankie was once again cited by the court for failure to pay child support. The court placed him on probation for three years and reduced his child support payments to $50 a month based on his earnings of that year, which were $2,901.14, plus $370 in unemployment benefits.

Of interest, the *Los Angeles Daily News* of August 16, 1951, reported Frankie had just opened a bar on Santa Monica Boulevard and had named it, "Try Later." Commenting on his choice of names for his bar, Frankie said, "You know when you call Central Casting, they tell you only two things on the phone, either 'no work,' or 'try later.'" Explaining why he decided to go into the bar business, Frankie replied, "I've spent so much money on the other side of the bar that I thought I'd get behind one and get even." The Try Later featured something called "The Sunday Morning Club" where hungry actors could get ham and eggs, potatoes, toast, coffee, and a drink for $1. Frankie commented, "But that's only if you're a member of the club. To be a member you've got to have a card and pay a dime. That's to keep out the riffraff."

Sometime during all these events, Frankie married for the third time. This time the bride was actress Dorothy Carroll. *Variety* reported on March 11, 1970, "Frankie Darro is off to Viet Nam as part of a USO unit."

Variety reported in its issue of December 28, 1976, "Frankie Darro, 59, one time child actor who bridged the gap into adult roles, died suddenly of a heart attack Christmas night while visiting friends in Huntington Beach. His wife Dorothy was with him at the time."

SUGAR DAWN

Born Mervelyn Sugar Steinberg on November 14, 1931, In San Francisco, she had juvenile roles in seven of the early B-westerns. Sugar had her own pony, Chiquita, as she rode the Hollywood range in THE GOLDEN TRAIL ('40) and PALS OF THE SILVER SAGE ('40) with Tex Ritter, and in DYNAMITE CANYON ('41), RIDING THE SUNSET TRAIL ('41), LONE STAR LAW MEN ('41), WANDERERS OF THE WEST ('41) and ARIZONA ROUNDUP ('42), all with Tom Keene.

Finally located after years of searching, Boyd Magers, publisher of *Western Clippings,* interviewed Sugar Dawn recently. He asked how she happened to begin riding at such a young age. Sugar replied: "From the San Francisco Zoo! I started on a mule at the zoo. My father put me on it all the time. I could ride very early, even before I could walk! We moved to the peninsula so I could have a pony, and my father could have a horse. His horse was 17 hands, and I rode that horse, too. I rode my pony Chiquita in horse shows at age 4 to 5, doing exhibitions, tricks. I put Chiquita through his paces. Taught it lots of tricks."

As for getting into pictures, Sugar explained, "I was at the '39 San Francisco World's Fair at Treasure Island. I performed on Chiquita under black light…I was seen by a lot of people, so I was requested to play Bonnie Blue Butler in GONE WITH THE WIND. I remember David O. Selznick, Clark Gable and Vivien Leigh. I had been fitted for contact lens and had my hair dyed to fit the part. Then, a politician from the South came in, saying the picture would not be shown in the South unless his niece played the part. So I was out. They wanted me to double for her in the riding scenes, but I refused! Years later, when I tested for the part of Velvet Brown, and lost to Elizabeth Taylor, they wanted me to double Elizabeth on Pi, but I also refused that. I had done too much by then to be an unbilled double!" As for Monogram, "Universal was going to write in a part for me in DESTRY RIDES AGAIN, but I fell off my pony and got a case of poison ivy. That kept me out of DESTRY, but, Robert Tansey at Monogram contacted my father about doing westerns, and that was how it began."

During and after her film career, Sugar did many charity benefits. She told Magers, "I did bond rallies and traveled with a captured Japanese sub, appeared at hospital wards, did many exhibitions and competitions at rodeos, and rode in the Rose Parade in '41. The hospital visits were very unique. I'd take my pony to the hospital, put rubber shoes on Chiquita, and go into the wards where the more critical children would be. We would perform for them and outside we could do more, tricks and things, for the kids who could come. I didn't ride inside-of course, but I performed tricks with Chiquita even after I was too big to ride on her." During the war, Sugar Dawn continued to perform. "I did a rodeo with Jane Withers; I did shows with Mickey Rooney and Judy Garland; Bonita Granville and Bob Hope. But I never kept in touch with anyone after it was over. But I did enjoy everything I did. I rode until the pony, or the horse, died. I can't recall which one went first."

Also to Magers, she related how she came by the name Sugar Dawn: "It's a long story. When Dr. Bone delivered me to my mother, she started to cry. Dr. Bone had to tell her 'She's not glass; she won't break. She's not butter; she won't melt. She's made of sugar, because she is sweet.'" As for the name Dawn, "My father was in the neon lighting business, which was new at the time, in San Francisco. The term 'dawning' is associated with neon lights, and that's where the second name of Dawn came. I still go by Sugar today!"

Also in Magers' interview: commenting on her co-stars, "Tom Keene was a very, very nice gentleman, a good rider, we had lots of fun. And the same can be said for Tex Ritter, who also had a good singing voice. We had lots of fun on those pictures. It wasn't like work or making movies, it was like playing, like make-believe. It was wonderful!" As for the leading ladies, "Betty Miles I remember well. She was a pretty lady, but they all were very pretty and very, very nice."

Sugar Dawn related that in '65, she married Loren Tower, a general manager for the largest carnival west of the Rockies. Together, they had a daughter named Dawn. The Towers traveled extensively in the carnival off-seasons. Sugar said that before Loren died in 1997, he told her to continue to travel, and that's what she has done: "I golf, swim and see the world. In November and December I took a cruise to the war islands of WWII, like Iwo Jima and Midway. As Loren died from a war-related illness, I was interested to see where he served. I was interviewed by representatives from the Library of Congress, after they found out about my war efforts, and it will become part of a WWII documentary, airing later this year on the History Channel." As for her latest travels, "I just returned from Antarctica. We were on an ice cutter; we did wet landings and walked among penguins, seals and icebergs, which have gorgeous colors. It's like a fairyland down there."

JOHNNY DUNCAN

Most fans associate Johnny Duncan with the role of "Robin" in the 1949 serial, BATMAN AND ROBIN, when he co-starred with Robert Lowery, who portrayed "Batman." Duncan also had three roles in westerns: one as a "Kid Kowboy" when he appeared in THE ARIZONA WILDCAT ('38) with Jane Withers and Leo Carrillo, another as a late teenager with Gene Autry in CALL OF THE CANYON ('42), and a third as an adult when he again supported Gene Autry in TRAIL TO SAN

ANTONE ('47).

Johnny's non-westerns are a varied lot. He appeared in two of the "Dead End Kids" series, COME OUT FIGHTING ('45) and FIGHTING FOOLS ('49). He joined the "Eastside Kids" in CLANCY STREET BOYS ('43), MILLION DOLLAR KID ('44), and MR. MUGGS RIDES AGAIN ('45). Among his other credits are roles in CAMPUS RHYTHM ('43) with Gale Storm, JIVE JUNCTION ('43) with Dickie Moore, DAVID AND BATHSHEBA ('51) with Gregory Peck, THE PRIDE OF ST. LOUIS ('52) with Dan Dailey, ALL ASHORE ('53) with Mickey Rooney, MISS SADIE THOMPSON ('53) with Rita Hayworth, THE CAINE MUTINY ('54) with Humphrey Bogart, ROCK AROUND THE CLOCK ('56) with Bill Haley and the Comets, and PLAN 9 FROM OUTER SPACE ('58), Bela Lugosi's final film. Duncan's final role, thankfully, was deleted, as he played a beheaded man in SPARTACUS ('60).

John Bowman Duncan, the only child of Robert L. Duncan and Melvina Duncan, was born on December 7, 1923, in Kansas City, Missouri. He spent most of his youth on an 80-acre farm north of Kansas City where the family eked out a living during the depression years. Johnny's father was also a barber who plied his trade every Saturday in a nearby town, literally giving a "shave and a haircut, two-bits." Johnny's mother supplemented the family's meager income by working as a beauty operator.

At age 9, Johnny taught himself to tap dance. On Saturdays when his father was barbering, Johnny was given a dime to go to the movies. However, rather than going to the movies, Johnny spent his time at the Sugar Bowl Bar tap dancing to tunes on the juke box where bar patrons would toss coins at his feet.

Johnny recalls a family meeting during the worst of the depression years. Both parents were crying, as they did not have the $125 to pay the annual mortgage on their farm, and were in fear of losing their home. Johnny then produced the money he had made tap dancing. It was more than enough to save the farm. Johnny says his father was, at first, angry and gave him a kick in the butt for keeping the money secret at a time the family was in dire straits, but then hugged him and started providing Johnny with tap dancing lessons from a teacher who charged 25 cents an hour. Thus, Johnny learned to professionally dance.

Johnny soon teamed up with a young girl, Lou Fisher, and the dance team of Duncan and Fisher performed together in the Kansas City area from 1933-1938. It was during a vaudeville performance in 1938 at the Tower Theatre in Kansas City that a talent scout from 20th Century Fox was in the audience and signed Johnny to a six-month contract at $50 a week. The family sold all their possessions, bought a new 1938 Chevrolet for $515, and was off to Hollywood.

Johnny says his favorite screen role was as "Robin" in the "Batman and Robin" serial and that his favorite actor is Humphrey Bogart. He names among his close friends in the entertainment industry Donald O'Connor, Audie Murphy and Jean Porter.

Johnny says his education consisted of 12 plus years of schooling. During World War II, Johnny served in the U. S. Navy aboard a submarine as a radioman. Following his acting career he served as vice-president of the Glen Ivy Resort in California, and then as vice-president at the Fall Creek Resort in Branson, Missouri.

Duncan's hobbies are golf and archery. He recalls spending evenings at a nine-hole municipal golf course playing with Bob Steele. He has won awards at archery and bodybuilding.

Duncan is currently married to his wife, Susan, an Indianapolis, Indiana, girl born on June 27, 1963. Johnny is the father of five: a daughter Cathy, 57, a son Sean, 22, a daughter Mandy, 17, a daughter Maranda, 13, and a son Landon, 8. He is also the grandfather of Danny Stevens, and is three times a great-grandfather. The Duncans now reside in Branson, Missouri.

JUNIOR DURKIN

In spite of his considerable talent, juvenile actor Junior Durkin appears to have suffered from an identity crisis among Hollywood writers. Several respected sources insist Durkin's true name was Trent Durkin. Others refer to him as James Durkin, possibly confusing him with another older player of the same era. However, a Paramount Pictures release of June 1931, states he was christened as Bernard Durkin, and that he was not a true junior. The moniker was only a nickname given to him by his family as a baby.

Durkin was born on July 2, 1915, in New York City. His father was the owner of hotels in both New York City and Philadelphia. His mother, formerly Florence Edwards, was a well-known actress. Junior had at least two sisters, Grace and Gertrude, both of whom were said to have been on stage since early childhood.

Much of Durkin's early success was accomplished on the New York stage. At age two-and-a half he appeared in the comedy musical "Some Night." By age five he was getting credited roles. One of these roles was the child in the revival of "The Squaw Man." At age six, he appeared in "H.M.S. Pinafore." This was followed by roles at age eight with Madge Kennedy and W. C. Fields in "Poppy," and at nine with Mary Nash in "The Lady." In 1928 he was cast for the part of "Bill" in "Courage," which ran for nearly a year on Broadway. This juvenile role was the lead opposite Janet Beecher, and metropolitan critics hailed Junior as an actor of the first rank.

Radio work and vaudeville kept Junior busy for the next couple of years. He appeared with his sister Gertrude in "The Little Vagabond" and was featured in radio acts over national hook-ups. His Hollywood debut occurred in 1930 in a film titled FAME. Paramount then signed him to appear with Richard Arlen in SPANISH ACRES, later re-titled THE SANTA FE TRAIL, where he shared juvenile honors with Mitzi Green.

Junior's "Kid Kowboy" roles were in Richard Arlen westerns, the most notable being THE SANTA FE TRAIL ('30). He is credited with Arlen in THE LAW RIDES WEST ('30), but this was a British version of THE SANTA FE TRAIL. Junior's one other western was THE CONQUERING HORDE ('31) with Arlen and Fay Wray. The zenith of Durkin's Hollywood career was reached during two films in which he co-starred with his best friend, Jackie Coogan—TOM SAWYER ('30) and HUCKLEBERRY FINN ('31). Coogan played "Sawyer," and Durkin played "Finn." Junior's final film roles were in 1934's LITTLE MEN, BIG HEARTED HERBERT, and CHASING YESTERDAY ('35).

Tragedy struck on May 4, 1935. A party of five was driving from the Imperial Valley in Jackie Coogan's new car. John Coogan, Jackie's father, was driving south of San Diego near the Mexican border when a speeding car with two women occupants approached them from the opposite direction and caused the Coogan car to swerve off the road and crash. Occupants of the Coogan car, in addition to John Coogan, were Robert J. Horner, a scenarist and writer, Charles Jones, foreman of the Coogan ranch, and in the rumble seat sat Jackie Coogan and his good friend, Junior Durkin. Jackie Coogan was thrown clear and survived. All four of the other occupants were killed.

Junior Durkin lies at rest at Forest Lawn in Glendale, California.

GEORGE ERNEST

George Ruud Hjorth was born November 30, 1921, in Pittsfield, Massachusetts. Arriving in Hollywood in the mid-1920s, where his first roles were in a couple of "Our Gang" comedy shorts, he wisely became George Ernest.

In a film career that included over fifty movie roles, George made four appearances as a "Kid Kowboy." In 1931 he supported Buck Jones in THE DEADLINE. The following year he had a role in the Tom Mix western DESTRY RIDES AGAIN. SONG OF THE SADDLE ('36) with Dick Foran, and THE PLAINSMAN ('36) with Gary Cooper closed out his juvenile roles in western films. He made one appearance in an oater as an adult supporting Gene Autry in STARDUST ON THE SAGE ('42).

Of Ernest's non-western films, he was best known for his numerous appearances in the "Jones Family" comedies playing one of the sons of Jed Prouty and Spring Byington. Among his other film credits are roles in UNION DEPOT ('32) with Joan Blondell and Douglas Fairbanks, Jr., HANDLE WITH CARE ('32) with James Dunn, FIREMAN SAVE MY CHILD ('32) with Joe E. Brown, THE HUMAN SIDE ('34) with Adolphe Menjou. LITTLE MEN ('35) with Ralph Morgan, DIAMOND JIM ('35) with Edward Arnold, THE TRAIL OF THE LONESOME PINE ('36) with Henry Fonda, PARADISE FOR THREE ('28) with Robert Young, BOY FRIEND ('39) with Jane Withers, FOUR SONS ('40) with Don Ameche, and MOUNTAIN MOONLIGHT ('41) with the Weaver Brothers and Elviry.

During World War II, George served with the OSS. Following the war, George worked for some thirty years with the McDonnell Douglas Space System Company in southern California as an engineer. Ernest is married and the father of two sons. He is now retired and living in Cypress, California.

EDITH FELLOWS

In a career in the world of entertainment that spanned over 70 years, Edith Fellows (all 4 feet, 10 inches of her) was another with roles as a "Kid Kowboy." Edith Marilyn Fellows was born in Boston, Massachusetts, on May 20, 1923, but grew up as the ward of her maternal grandmother in

Hollywood. Edith's mother disappeared when Edith was two years old. As to what next occurred, accounts vary. One source reports that Edith's father was offered a job in North Carolina and took Edith with him. This was the only reference to Edith's father that was found. Yet another source has Edith's grandmother traveling to Massachusetts to pick up Edith and bring her to North Carolina. In any event, Edith did end up living with her grandmother.

By 1926, Edith was excelling in dance school when she was noticed by an "agent" who urged her grandmother to bring Edith to Hollywood. Edith and her grandmother made the trip to Hollywood only to discover that the "agent's" address was a vacant lot. They decided to remain in Hollywood where the grandmother obtained work as a domestic. Authors Michael G. Fitzgerald and Boyd Magers, in their book *Ladies of the Western*, report that a neighbor, whose young boy was an actor, was caring for Edith one day when the boy was called by Hal Roach Studios for a part. Allegedly, Edith accompanied them to the studio where, after getting the part, the boy developed measles, and Edith was selected to replace him.

Edith made her film debut in 1929 and appeared in three "Our Gang" comedy shorts. Her western films began with an un-credited role in CIMARRON ('31) with Richard Dix. As a juvenile, she later had parts in THE RIDER OF DEATH VALLEY ('32) with Tom Mix, and in LAW AND LAWLESS ('32) with Jack Hoxie and Wally Wales. In 1942 Edith made appearances with Gene Autry in HEART OF THE RIO GRANDE and STARDUST ON THE STAGE.

Among her non-western credits are roles in DADDY LONG LEGS ('31) with Janet Gaynor, HUCKLEBERRY FINN ('31) with Jackie Coogan and Junior Durkin, THE DEVIL'S BROTHER ('33) with Laurel and Hardy, JANE EYRE ('34) with Virginia Bruce, MRS. WIGGS OF THE CABBAGE PATCH ('34) with W. C. Fields, SHE MARRIED HER BOSS ('35) with Claudette Colbert, PENNIES FROM HEAVEN ('36) with Bing Crosby, and in four of the "Five Little Peppers" series: FIVE LITTLE PEPPERS AND HOW THEY GREW ('39), FIVE LITTLE PEPPERS AT HOME ('40), FIVE LITTLE PEPPERS IN TROUBLE ('40), and OUT WEST WITH THE PEPPERS ('40), in which she had the starring roles.

Apparently learning of Edith's success, in 1936 the mother who had abandoned her showed up and demanded custody. The grandmother refused, and a long and bitter court custody battle ensued. The grandmother was victorious and remained Edith's caretaker.

In the mid-1940s, Edith left Hollywood for several decades where she embraced other avenues in the entertainment world. She appeared in Broadway musicals, did stock shows on the road, and entered the newly-arrived world of television. Her television roles included "Between Two Brothers" ('82), "Grace Kelly Story" ('83), "The Hills Have Eyes Part II" ('85) and "The Pursuit of Happiness" ('95). Edith made guest appearances on several of television's popular shows including "Studio One," "Simon & Simon," "Father Murphy," "Scarecrow and Mrs. King," and "E. R."

Edith Fellows has been twice married. In 1946 she married Freddie Fields, a producer-agent. This marriage produced a daughter, Kathy Lynn Fields, in 1947. Edith and Freddie divorced in 1955. Daughter Kathy spent most of her growing-up years with Freddie and his new wife, Polly Bergen. Kathy later became an actress and married actor David Lander.

In 1962, Edith walked down the aisle a second time, as she reportedly wed Hal Lee. No word as to whether this union endured or if there were other children.

At last reports, Edith was still going strong, as she played herself in a 2000 production, I USED TO BE IN PICTURES, a never-released documentary.

BILLY GRAY

Billy Gray is personable, interesting, and an "up-front, tell it like it is" kind of person. *(My kind of guy.)*

William Thomas Gray was born in Los Angeles on January 13, 1938. His father was also named William Gray, but the two were apparently not close because when Billy was asked about his father's occupation, his reply was "unknown." Billy's mother is another story. The former Beatrice Kimbrough, who later became B-western heroine Beatrice Gray, is a lady of class and talent and is still doing award-winning television commercials in her eighties. Beatrice Gray honored the author by writing one of the forewords to an earlier book, *Bob Steele, His "Reel" Women.* She was twice Bob Steele's leading lady. I first met the Grays at the Asheville Film Festival where Beatrice was one of the invited guests. She was accompanied by her son Billy, and both proved to be popular with the festival crowd.

Billy Gray had three siblings. A brother Franklin, six years older than Billy, was an architect who designed the Honolulu International Airport terminal (a beautiful structure that I have visited hundreds of times). A second brother, Fred, ten years younger than Billy, attended U.C.L.A. on a basketball scholarship. Sister Gloria, seven years older than Billy, is deceased. Education-wise, Billy completed one year at Los Angeles Community College.

Billy's film career covered a span of thirty-seven years, commencing in 1943 when he made his initial appearance in MAN OF COURAGE with Barton MacLane, and ending with a role in PORKLIPS NOW ('80). During this period, he is credited with forty-six movies, five of which qualify as "Kid "Kowboy" roles. Among his non-western credits are such well-received movies as FIGHTING FATHER DUNNE ('48), JIM THORPE-ALL AMERICAN ('51), and SEVEN LITTLE FOYS ('55).

Billy's western films consisted of juvenile support in BAD MEN OF TOMBSTONE ('49) with Barry Sullivan, SINGING GUNS ('50) with Vaughn Monroe, SIERRA PASSAGE ('50) with Wayne Morris, GENE AUTRY AND THE MOUNTIES ('51), and OUTLAW STALLION ('54) with Phil Carey.

When asked his favorite role, Billy replied, "Bobby Benson" in THE DAY THE EARTH STOOD STILL ('51). He also made several guest appearances in western television shows. Billy is credited with two "Gene Autry Show" ('50) roles. He is further credited as part of the cast in a "Cheyenne" ('55), a "The Deputy" ('59), and a "Rawhide" ('59). Contrary to what certain writers have reported, Billy says, "I was never in TWO FOR THE SEESAW and SOME LIKE IT HOT."

His two favorite performances in the industry and the actor credited therein, Billy says, "Emil

Jannings in THE BLUE ANGEL and Laurence Olivier in THE ENTERTAINER were the greatest." When I asked him to discuss some of the highlights relating to his entertainment days, Billy listed two events: he was nominated for an Emmy, television's highest award, for his role as Bud Anderson in the series, "Father Knows Best"; and in July 1998 he settled a libel suit he had filed against film critic, Leonard Maltin, who annually issues guides on available movies and videos. In Maltin's guides from 1974 to 1998, he had referred to Billy as a real-life drug addict and pusher in his critique of the 1971 film, DUSTY AND SWEETS MCGEE, a film in which Billy had a role as an actor. Maltin was in error. In his suit Billy demanded that he issue a public apology for a twenty-seven-year-long defamation of character. Maltin did so at a press conference on July 18, 1998.

Billy listed Dean Stockwell, Bobby Blake, Bobby Driscoll, Russ Tamblyn, Robert Wise, and Jane Wyatt as his closest friends in the industry.

Following the end of his acting career, Billy raced Class "A" Speedway motorcycles for 23 years, often three to five nights a week. He comments, "I beat the world champ once." In 1975 he promoted a series of races at the Bakersfield County Fairgrounds in Bakersfield, California. He says his hobby is inventing and has acquired several patents. Among his creations on the market are a jack-o-lantern candleholder, guitar picks, guitar pick holder, guitar strap lock, a back massager, and a champagne cork remover.

As to his domestic life, Billy says he has been married three times and that each of his ventures in wedlock lasted for one year. But, he commented, "They were all beautiful." In 1961 he was married in Italy to Paola Quarguali, a professor of Italian. In 1968 in California, he married Helena Kallioniotes. Billy says that Helena was a restaurateur, an actress, and a belly dancer. Billy made his third and final trip down the aisle in 1980 when he married Donna Wilkes, an actress.

Billy Gray is living the good life today in Topanga Canyon, California.

GARY GRAY

Baseball's Leo Durocher once commented, "Nice guys finish last." Obviously, Durocher never met Gary Gray. Gary Gray is one of the world's "nice guys" and a winner to all who know him.

Gary was the only son of Bill Gray, a business manager for many of Hollywood's elite, and Jeanie Ellen Dickson. A second child, a daughter Arlene, born in 1938, also had a career in the world of entertainment as an actress, dancer, and model.

Born Gary Dickson Gray on December 18, 1936, in Los Angeles, Gary owes his start in films as a juvenile player to comments made by two of Hollywood's major personalities, Jack Benny and Bert Wheeler. Upon meeting three-year-old Gary, Benny and Wheeler (both clients of Gray's father, Bill) commented, "This kid ought to be in pictures." Gary's parents took the comments seriously and following a successful screen test, Gary made his debut as a three-and-a-half year-old, unbilled member of the cast of A WOMAN'S FACE ('41), starring Joan Crawford.

Prior to 1947, several of Gray's roles were unbilled, but the films are quality films such as SUN VALLEY SERENADE ('41), HEAVEN CAN WAIT ('43), and GASLIGHT ('44). His first billed role was in the 1944 film ADDRESS UNKNOWN starring Paul Lukas and K. P. Stevens. Earlier he had appeared in the Jackie Cooper film, WHERE ARE YOUR CHILDREN? ('43). Included in that cast are two of B-westerns' future heroines, Gale Storm and Evelyn Eaton. Also joining Gary as part of that film's cast were his sister, Arlene Gray, and Eilene Janssen.

Two 1948-released films did much to enhance Gary's career as a "Kid Kowboy" and his stature as an actor. He had a prominent role as "Young Johnny" in the big budget RKO western, RETURN OF THE BAD MEN starring Randolph Scott, and which included in the cast such B-western luminaries as Gabby Hayes, Tom Keene, and Tom Tyler. Later that same year, Gary played the role he says is the favorite of all the roles played in his twenty-year career—the role of "Young Davey" in the Loretta Young/William Holden classic, RACHEL AND THE STRANGER.

Since this book is about the juvenile players who brought us joy in their roles in westerns, it's time to reflect on the Gary Gray in the Saturday afternoon "shoot 'em ups." While Gary had roles in several other western films, his B-westerns are pretty much limited to two appearances in which he had roles in support of Tim Holt and Richard Martin in GUN SMUGGLERS ('48) and MASKED RAIDERS ('49).

During his versatile career, Gary had feature roles that he shared with some of Hollywood's canine stars. He worked with Ace the Wonder Dog, the fabled Lassie, and in a myriad of films with Flame. Of all his four-footed co-stars, Gary says Flame possessed the most talent. Gary's final film was the 1962 release TERROR AT BLACK FALLS, in which he had top billing with House Peters, Jr.

There are also many television credits during Gary's storied twenty-year career in entertainment. The variety of the different roles that Gary played in these episodes only added to his stature as an actor as he made his mark in fantasy shows ("Captain Midnight"), historical dramas ("The Boston Tea Party"), sports ("The Jackie Jensen Story") comedy ("I Love Lucy") and westerns ("Annie Oakley"). Gary's final television role was with Hugh O'Brian in a 1960 "Wyatt Earp" episode.

Gary's formal education was not neglected in spite of the demands of his heavy schedule. He attended not only the studio school provided for young actors, but also graduated from Van Nuys Junior High School and Van Nuys High School, and spent two years at Valley Junior College. Adding another dimension to his many talents, Gary excelled in the sports of gymnastics and diving.

From 1955 to 1961, Gary was a member of the California Air National Guard. From 1961-1962, he was on active duty as a member of the United States Air Force and served in the Air Force Reserves from 1962 to 1964, attaining the rank of staff sergeant.

Disproving the adage that opposites attract, on January 28, 1961, at Burbank, California, "nice guy" Gary Gray married "nice gal" Jean Bean, a California girl. This union continues until this day and has produced four daughters: Cindy Jean, April Lyn, Kimberly Ann, and Carrie Elizabeth. These four young ladies, all married, have blessed the Gray household with nineteen grandchildren. As a nice touch, two of the grandsons are named Gary.

After leaving the entertainment business, Gary worked in various capacities with several firms in the swimming pool industry. He retired in 1999 after a 39-year career. Jean is still working as a bridal consultant, although she manages to find time to accompany Gary on his frequent appearances at film festivals where he is among the more popular guest celebrities.

How does Gary like to spend his time now? "Golf, photography, family, travel, and film festivals," he replied. He is also a collector of tapes of his movies and television shows, as well as stills, posters and lobby cards from his time in Hollywood.

When asked to name his favorite performers, one might have expected Gary to name some of the western stars. He surprised me by naming Bill Holden, Natalie Wood, Tom Hanks, and Meg Ryan. His favorite western players were Tim Holt, Bob Steele, and Gabby Hayes. He also commented that another favorite "probably because I worked with him several times and he was one of the really good guys who most often played a bad guy," is I. Stanford Jolley—not a star but a great cowboy character actor."

Asked to name his closest friends from his Hollywood days, he replied, "There are too many to list." *Knowing Gary, this response brings to mind a comment by another movie cowboy in one of his films: "You better believe it, pilgrim."*

KAROLYN GRIMES

Many only recall Karolyn Grimes as the cute six-year-old who spoke the memorable line, "Every time a bell rings, an angel gets his wings," in her role as Zuzu Bailey, the daughter of James Stewart and Donna Reed, in the classic film IT'S A WONDERFUL LIFE ('46). However, she was also one of the "Kid Kowboys," as she graced four westerns during her brief career. Her support roles in western films included appearances in UNCONQUERED ('47) with Gary Cooper and Paulette Goddard, ALBUQUERQUE ('48) with Randolph Scott, LUST FOR GOLD ('49) with Glenn Ford and Ida Lupino, and RIO GRANDE ('50) with John Wayne.

Karolyn's non-western credits during her seven-year, 16-film career, include roles in THAT NIGHT WITH YOU ('45) with Franchot Tone, PARDON MY PAST ('46) with Fred MacMurray, BLUE SKIES ('46) with Bing Crosby and Fred Astaire, SISTER KENNY ('46) with Rosalind Russell, MOTHER WORE TIGHTS ('47) with Betty Grable, HONEYCHILE ('51) with Judy Canova, and her final film, HANS CHRISTIAN ANDERSEN ('52) with Danny Kaye. Her two most noteworthy roles—which incidentally were her favorite films—were IT'S A WONDERFUL LIFE, where juvenile players Jimmy Hawkins, Larry Simms, and Carol Coombes were part of the cast, and THE BISHOP'S WIFE ('47) with Cary Grant and Loretta Young.

Karolyn was born on July 4, 1940, in Hollywood. Despite her success as a young actress, Karolyn's life had its tragic moments. Both of her parents died while she was still a teenager. Notwithstanding the sorrow caused by the loss of her mother and father, these events also resulted in an end to what might have been a continuing acting career. Grimes was sent to live with an aunt and uncle in Missouri. These relatives felt that Hollywood was a depraved place and saw to it that all contacts with it by Karolyn were terminated. It wasn't until many years later that Karolyn was able to return to reunite with friends and visit the scenes of her early triumphs. In 1993 she returned to join Hawkins, Simms, and Coombs in a holiday tour sponsored by Target Stores.

There were other low spots in life's road for Karolyn. She lost both her first husband and a son to death. But things have since improved. Grimes now lives in Stilwell, Kansas, just outside of Kansas City, with her husband of over 25 years, Mike Wilkerson, a contractor. Together they have raised a family of seven children, five of whom were from earlier marriages. She is active in community theater and speaks before groups about her time spent filming IT'S A WONDERFUL LIFE. "I love it," she says, "I carry pictures from the film in my purse and sign them when people ask."

Of IT'S A WONDERFUL LIFE, she says, "I love that movie. A lot of adverse things have happened. But there are balances out there. And the movie itself has affected my life so much, because I have George Bailey's philosophy...that friendships and caring and loving will carry you through anything. And I believe in that. If I didn't, I think I would have collapsed by now."

In 2001, Karolyn played herself in the television special "Spotlight on Karolyn Grimes." She is currently working to publish an IT'S A WONDERFUL LIFE cookbook.

JIMMY HAWKINS

Jimmy Hawkins' achievements in the world of entertainment are impressive. Equally impressive are his contributions to others. Most impressive on screen was his co-starring role as "Tagg Oakley" in the television series "Annie Oakley."

Jimmy was born in Los Angeles on November 13, 1941. His father, Tommie Hawkins, was born in South Dakota and was one of the original "Keystone Kops" who later worked as a prop man. His mother, Bette, a Los Angeles native, worked as an extra. Jimmy said she had to be present while he was working, so the studio decided she was a prime candidate for work; her extra roles were numerous. Jimmy has two siblings, a sister Sue and a brother Tim. Tim had a role in CATTLE DRIVE ('51).

Hawkins made his screen debut at age three with a part in THE SEVENTH CROSS ('44) with Spencer Tracy. In the years that followed, he had roles in films with many of Hollywood's legends. Included among his credits are MARRIAGE IS A PRIVATE AFFAIR ('44) with Lana Turner and John Hodiak, the blockbuster IT'S A WONDERFUL LIFE ('46) portraying the young son of Jimmy Stewart in a film that included such other luminaries as Donna Reed and Lionel Barrymore, THE SEA OF GRASS ('47) with Spencer Tracy and Katharine Hepburn, MOONRISE ('48) with Dane Clark and Gail Russell, BODYGUARD ('48) with Lawrence Tierney, CAUGHT ('49), and CHAL-LENGE TO LASSIE ('49). Other juvenile roles continued with parts in THE FORSYTH SAGA ('49) with Errol Flynn and Greer Garson, HOLIDAY AFFAIR ('49) with Robert Mitchum and Janet Leigh, LOVE THAT BRUTE ('50) with Paul Douglas and Jean Peters, NEVER A DULL MOMENT ('50) with Fred MacMurray and Irene Dunne, STRICTLY DISHONORABLE ('51) with Ezio Pinza and Janet Leigh, JIM THORPE - ALL AMERICAN ('51) with Burt Lancaster, MISTER SCOUTMASTER ('53) with Clifton Webb, YANKEE PASHA ('54) with Jeff Chandler and Rhonda Fleming, and PRIVATE HELL 36 ('54) with Ida Lupino.

Jimmy's films as a "Kid Kowboy" included WINCHESTER 73 ('50) with Jimmy Stewart and Shelly Winters, THE WOMAN THEY ALMOST LYNCHED ('53) with John Lund and Joan Leslie, SAVAGE FRONTIER ('53) with Allan Lane and Bob Steele, DESTRY ('54) with Audie Murphy, and COUNT THREE AND PRAY ('55) with Van Heflin.

As an adult, Jimmy's "big screen" roles were limited. He and Tom Poston appeared together in ZOTZ ('62), and he twice shared billings with Elvis Presley in GIRL HAPPY ('65) and SPINOUT ('56).

Hollywood films were only a small part of Jimmy's successes in the world of entertainment. His roles in television series were many and include "The Ruggles" ('49), "Annie Oakley" ('54), "Dennis the Menace" ('63), "The Adventures of Ozzie and Harriet" ('61), "Leave It To Beaver" ('61), "Ichabod and Me" ('61), "Margie" ('61), "The Donna Reed Show" ('63), "Gidget" ('65), and "Petticoat Junction" ('66). He served as the creator and writer of "Love Leads the Way" ('84) and "Motown Returns to the Apollo" ('85), both television specials.

Jimmy served as producer of several television documentaries including "Evel Knievel" ('71), "Scout's Honor" ('80), "A Time For Miracles" ('80), and "Merry Christmas, George Bailey" ('97). He was also the producer of the highly-acclaimed television story of the fabled Negro League baseball legend who was long denied his place in organized professional baseball, "Don't Look Back: The Story of LeRoy 'Satchel' Paige" ('81).

Hawkins received his education at private schools—he attended Holy Trinity School and graduated from Notre Dame High School in Thousand Oaks, California. He was a golfer in high school.

Jimmy has never married, but a story he related to the author recently lends some insight into what sort of person he is. Now a busy sixty-plus-years-old, he said, "I'm a Mister Mom." A niece with an infant child was involved with serious personal problems, so Jimmy took over the responsibility of caring for the child.

Jimmy Hawkins has devoted much if his "spare" time to a variety of endeavors, most of them designed to benefit others. In his productions he has attempted to find roles for juvenile actors of the past saying, "Most child stars don't stay in the industry, but people want to know what happened to them." He is a long-time member of the Donna Reed Foundation, which awards scholarships in the performing arts. He has visited with—and performed for—American servicemen and women in such far away places as Viet Nam for the USO.

Hawkins has received awards and citations from the Department of State, the N.A.A.C.P., and a Lifetime Achievement Award for Kid Actors for his work. He served in the California Air National Guard for six years.

Jimmy says much of his philosophy was learned at the knee of Gene Autry. The two visited hospitals while on tour, gave autographs at baseball games, and attended charity functions. Mr. Autry always told me, "We have to give back."

Others have also influenced Hawkins' life. He says, "I was fortunate enough to have had the rare pleasure to have been hired by Ozzie Nelson to appear regularly on 'The Adventures of Ozzie and Harriet.' They were very caring and involved people. They touched many lives on and off the television screen."

Jimmy's favorite roles were in the television series "Annie Oakley," where he was a regular as Tagg Oakley, the film IT'S A WONDERFUL LIFE, and his two movies with Elvis. His favorite performers were Donna Reed and Fred MacMurray. Today, his closest friend from the past is Shelley Fabares.

In 1992 Jimmy and fellow actor Paul Petersen co-authored the book *The "It's a Wonderful Life" Trivia Book*, and in 1997 he wrote *It's a Wonderful Life 50th Anniversary Scrapbook*, copies of which are sold at charity auctions.

Jimmy is a sports fan with baseball being his first love. Today Jimmy has his own business, The Jimmy Hawkins Company, in Los Angeles.

Count Jimmy Hawkins among Hollywood's nice people.

BUZZ HENRY

In a career cut short by tragedy, Buzz Henry managed to accomplish quite a lot. Among his over fifty cinema roles, many were in juvenile support roles for a number of the B-western cowboy stars. His first film was at the age of four in WESTERN FRONTIER ('35) with Ken Maynard. Next was a series of three Bob Allen oaters: UNKNOWN RANGER ('36), RIO GRANDE RANGER ('36) and RANGER COURAGE ('37). He next teamed up with Dave O'Brien for BUZZY RIDES THE RANGE ('40) and BUZZY AND THE PHANTOM PINTO ('41) These were followed by another nine cowboy flicks, RIDIN' DOWN THE CANYON ('42) with Roy Rogers, CALLING WILD BILL ELLIOTT ('43) with Bill Elliott, TRAIL TO GUNSIGHT ('44) with Eddie Dew, TRIGGER TRAIL ('44) with Rod Cameron, WILD BEAUTY ('46) with Lois Collier and Don Porter, WILD WEST ('46) with Eddie Dean, KING OF THE WILD HORSES ('47) with Preston Foster, LAW OF THE CANYON ('47) with Charles Starrett, and LAST OF THE REDMEN ('47) with Jon Hall.

During these juvenile years, Buzz had roles in three serials—ROARING WEST ('35) with Buck Jones, TEX GRANGER ('48) with Robert Kellard and pretty Peggy Stewart, and HOP HARRIGAN ('46) with William Bakewell and Jennifer Holt.

Entering his adult years, Buzz continued with roles in westerns, many of them quality films. Some of his later roles include ROCKY MOUNTAIN ('50) with Errol Flynn, HEART OF THE ROCKIES ('51) with Roy Rogers, THE HOMESTEADERS ('53) with Bill Elliott, LAST OF THE PONY RIDERS ('53) with Gene Autry, THE OUTCAST ('54) with John Derek and Bob Steele. THE INDIAN FIGHTER ('55) with Kirk Douglas, THE LAWLESS EIGHTIES ('57) with Buster Crabbe, THE SHEEPMAN ('58) and COWBOY ('58) both with Glenn Ford, SHENANDOAH ('65) with James Stewart, and EL DORADO ('67) with John Wayne. Henry also had one adult serial role,

THE MAN WITH THE STEEL WHIP ('54) that starred Richard Simmons. Buzz's final film was WATERHOLE #3 ('67).

Buzz managed to work in quite a few television guest appearances with roles on "Adventures of Wild Bill Hickok," "Buffalo Bill, Jr.," "The Adventures of Champion," "Annie Oakley," "Broken Arrow," "Zane Grey Theater" and "The Rounders."

Henry's Hollywood pursuits included more than acting. He served as part of the crew for special action sequences and as a technical advisor for WATERHOLE #3, IN LIKE FLINT ('67), OUR MAN FLINT ('65) and THE ROUNDERS ('65). He was stunt co-ordinator for OUR MAN FLINT, TEXAS ACROSS THE RIVER ('66) and MACKENNA'S GOLD ('69). Henry then worked up the ladder to become a second unit director in OUR MAN FLINT, THE WILD BUNCH ('69), MA-CHO CALLAHAN ('70) and THE COWBOYS ('72).

During lulls in his film career, Buzz spent time barnstorming on the rodeo circuit. He was one of the few "Kid Kowboys" who actually was a skilled rider. His ambition was to become a director, and in 1968 he spent time in New Guinea and Jamaica filming sequences toward that end.

Born in Colorado as Robert Dee Henry on September 4, 1931, the son of Robert Henry and Delia Alston, Buzz's promising career came to a tragic end at age 40 on September 30, 1971 as a result of an automobile accident that was the end result of a drag race. The report of the accident causing Henry's death states "driver auto struck auto" at Zoo Drive and Riverside that resulted in a fracture of the skull from blunt force trauma.

Buzz was married to Patricia M. Foley. At the time of his death, he was residing at 4601 Sancola, Toluca Lake, California, and was employed by Warner Brothers as a director. Buzz Henry is buried at Mission Cemetery in Mission Hills, California.

TIM HOLT

Tim Holt, son of legendary early silent screen western star Jack Holt, and the brother of western heroine, Jennifer Holt, was born Charles John Holt, III, on February 5, 1919, in Beverly Hills, California. Contrary to what many sources claim, he was not the brother of actor David Holt.

Tim appeared in a multitude of B-westerns as the star during his adult years, but one, and possibly three, of his oaters makes him eligible as a "Kid Kowboy." He first appeared in movies in THE VANISHING PIONEER ('28) with his father in the starring role. His two other possible juvenile western roles (although more probably as a late teenager or young adult) were in THE LAW WEST OF TOMBSTONE ('38) with Harry Carey, and THE RENEGADE RANGER ('38) with George O'Brien. We say these two films were possible juvenile roles because accepting the 1919 birthday would have made Tim 18 or 19 years of age during filming. (The 1919 birth date is considered reliable as that is the date reported in author Bobby Copeland's book, *B-Western Boot Hill* and in *Tim Holt* by David Rothel. However, various other sources give an earlier date of birth for Holt, and relying on Hollywood birth dates is tantamount to "rolling the dice.")

During his 149-film career that ended with an appearance in THIS STUFF'LL KILL YA! ('71), the majority of Holt's films are in B-westerns. However, there are some notable exceptions. Tim had a role with Barbara Stanwyck and John Boles in STELLA DALLAS ('38). The following year he appeared with John Wayne and Claire Trevor in STAGECOACH. These were followed by THE MAGNIFICENT AMBERSONS ('42) with Joseph Cotten and Anne Baxter, and the lead role in what was supposed to be a film of little consequence but received great reviews, HITLER'S CHILDREN ('42), where he was joined by Bonita Granville.

Holt's next two "A" film roles were probably career highlights for him. He joined Henry Fonda as one of the Earp brothers in what many say is the best of the "O.K. Corral" westerns, MY DARLING CLEMENTINE ('46), and he worked with Humphrey Bogart in THE TREASURE OF THE SIERRA MADRE ('46), a film in which his father, Jack Holt, had a bit role.

At least a portion of Tim's early education was obtained at Culver Military Academy. There was a three-year hiatus in Tim's movie life during World War II as he served in the U.S. Air Force as a bombardier.

Some Tim Holt trivia:

• Hollywood claimed that in the 1940s Tim had the "fastest draw" in films, saying he had the ability to draw his revolver in slightly over one-sixth of a second. *Maybe. But Hollywood is filled with claims of its B-western cowboys being rodeo champions when in actuality some would have had problems on a merry-go-round.*

• Tim was awarded the Distinguished Flying Cross for his service during World War II.

• Tim was three times married. His first two marriages, to Virginia Ashcroft and to Alice Harrison, ended in divorce. His third visit to the altar with Birdie Stephens endured.

• Tim fathered four children: a daughter, Bryanna, and three sons, Lance, Jack and Jay.

• Following Hollywood, Tim did some ranching and worked as a sales manager for radio station KEBC-FM in Oklahoma City.

• Tim Holt passed away from cancer at the Shawnee Medical Center Clinic in Shawnee, Oklahoma, on February 16, 1973. He lies at rest in an unmarked grave at Memory Lane in Harrah, Oklahoma.

JIMMY HOUSE

Jimmy House, a younger brother of the more famous "Kid Kowboy" Newton House, was himself one of the juvenile players who had roles in early western films. Personal contacts with several surviving members of the House clan, including Jimmy's sisters Lucille and Geraldine, brother Don, and Newton's son Charles and his wife, proved to be the only sources of information on the life and times of Jimmy House.

James Vernon House appeared in a supporting role to Buck Jones in WHITE EAGLE ('32). Family members are in agreement than the majority of films in which Jimmy appeared were in extra roles, or un-credited parts, although they recall that he had a good part in ARIZONA ('40) with Jean Arthur and William Holden.

According to sister Geraldine, Jimmy was born in Holly, Colorado, on February 23, 1917, although, sister Lucille thinks it was a few years later than 1917. According to the Social Security Database House was born November 3, 1921, in Mesa, Colorado. Jimmy graduated from Glendale's Hoover High School in 1937 and later attended Glendale Community College. During World War II, Jimmy spent four years in the Air Force as a bomber pilot. When asked about his rank, Lucille said, "He had some kind of silver bird on his shoulder," (lieutenant colonel), and brother Don said, "I think he was a lieutenant." Following the war, Jimmy returned to Hollywood, and worked for many years as a make-up artist, as did his brother Newton and Newton's son Charles. Later in life, Jimmy joined his brother Newton in the grain business and in raising racehorses.

Jimmy was married to Jeanne Swaisgood for 56 years. The couple had two sons—Tim, now deceased, and Ron, who is in the surfboard manufacturing business in San Juan Capistrano, California.

Jimmy House passed away on January 14, 1998. The cause and details of Jimmy's death were not discussed, as sister Lucille said, "He was my favorite, and even talking about it is too painful."

The House family is part of a rich history with its Hollywood connections. In addition to the contributions of Newton and Jimmy House, there were others:

- Jack House, the father, was both an actor and stuntman. Jack passed away on November 29, 1963, at age 76.

- There was an earlier Newton House, an uncle of Jack's. He was an early actor, and later a rancher in Baja, California. This Newton was born in Texas on January 10, 1865, and died on December 16, 1948.

- Don House, brother of Newton and Jimmy, was an actor and one of the busiest of Hollywood's stuntmen. Don resides in Santa Ynez, California.

- Sister Dorothy House appeared briefly in films before becoming the wife of western sidekick, Andy Devine. Dorothy passed away on February 18, 1977, at age 70.

- Sister Lucille, now in her nineties and residing in Los Angeles, had a film career as an actress and stuntwoman. She says her best friend in the industry is Maureen O'Hara, with whom she sometimes resides. She was O'Hara's stunt double and says that her favorite role was in MCLINTOCK where she did the falling down the stairs scene for O'Hara. Asked if she was the one "spanked' by John Wayne, she says that was O'Hara. Asked if she knew Bob Steele who was part of the film's cast, she answered that she did indeed know and remember him.

- Youngest sister, Geraldine, now in her seventies and living in Burbank, is the only one of the House children who had no association with the film industry.

NEWTON HOUSE

Charles Newton House was born on November 1, 1911, in Holly, Colorado. There is little information on Newton's early years, but it is obvious that he was raised in an environment that allowed him to be an accomplished rider and roper by the time he reached Hollywood in the early 1920s.

Newton's father, Charles C. "Jack" House, born in Texas, was a rancher. His mother, Candace L. Drope, was from Canada. *The Motion Picture Blu-Book*, 1930, has a notation that the boy was educated at the Rockwell grade school in Holly, Colorado.

For the trek west, the parents, Newton, his brothers Don and Jimmy, and sisters Lucille and Dorothy, left Colorado with $25.00 and 35 horses, and made their way to the Glendale area of California. (Another sister, Geraldine, was born after the family arrived in California.) After reaching California, the father opened a horse stable and became a stuntman and actor. The stable was originally a riding stable, but later began supplying horses to various studios for western movies.

Young Newton enrolled in the Los Angeles Professional School for Actors, and through his father's business connections with the studios, soon began getting juvenile movie roles. Newton's first screen roles were in 1924 with support roles in two non-westerns, THE SPIRIT OF THE U.S.A. and WHICH SHALL IT BE? His first western support role as a "Kid Kowboy" was also in 1924 in THE RIDIN' KID FROM POWDER RIVER with Hoot Gibson as the star. House also supported Gibson in, THE BUCKAROO KID ('26). He continued to play support roles until 1927 when Universal signed him to star in a series of two-reelers, "The Champion Boy Rider Series." This move by Universal was probably to compete with RKO's popular Buzz Barton series. The films were House's chief claim to fame as a young western player. Among the titles are THE RIDING WHIRLWIND, THE RED WARNING, CLEARING THE TRAIL, THE RACING WIZARD all in 1927, RIDING GOLD, BUCKSKIN DAYS, WINGED HOOFS, A SON OF THE FRONTIER, THE UNTAMED, THE FIGHTING KID, THE RIDE FOR HELP, ROPIN' ROMANCE, and THE DANGER TRAIL, all in 1928. Newton House has one serial to his credit, first billing in the 1929 Universal serial, A FINAL RECKONING, which also starred Buffalo Bill, Jr. (Jay Wilsey) and Louise Lorraine.

With the coming of sound and House about to enter his twenties, there were no juvenile parts for him, but he continued to remain active for a few years in various support roles. In 1930 he played a pony express rider in the Ann Harding version of GIRL OF THE GOLDEN WEST. This was followed by an un-credited role in 1934's, WE LIVE AGAIN, starring Fredric March, in which he plays a footman. In 1935 House had an un-credited role as an officer in the James Cagney/Pat O'Brien film, DEVIL DOGS OF THE AIR, and later played stand-in for Charles Boyer in BREAK OF HEARTS. It all ended in 1947 when House had his final appearance in another un-credited role when he joined pretty Peggy Stewart in SON OF ZORRO.

After leaving films, Newton worked from 1936 until 1947 as a Hollywood make-up artist. House left Hollywood and moved to Colton, California, where he operated House Grain & Feed and later raised racehorses on his Circle J-N Ranch until his retirement in 1982.

Newton was one time married, but was later divorced. The couple had two sons, Charles, who resides in Canoga Park, California, and James, who lives on Maui in Hawaii. Newton was not an easy person to get along with in his old age, and the family was not always on good terms. Finally, in his last years, he moved in with son Charles and his wife, and some wounds healed.

Newton House passed away on July 23, 1987, at age 75. He was survived by his two sons, two brothers, and three sisters. Newton died at home from cardiac failure after being a victim of heart disease for the final six months of his life. His remains were cremated and his ashes were placed at Mountain View Cemetery in San Bernardino, California.

A note of interest: among items of memorabilia from Newton's movie career, now possessed by son Charles and his wife, are two of Newton's contracts that called for payment of $75.00 per week.

JIMMY HUNT

Jimmy Hunt was another of the Hollywood juvenile players who appeared in western films. The first of his oaters was in support of Forrest Tucker and Adele Mara in ROCK ISLAND TRAIL ('50). In that same year he is credited with two more westerns, SADDLE TRAMP with Joel McCrea and Wanda Hendrix and THE CAPTURE with Lew Ayres and Teresa Wright. His final "shoot 'em up" was again with Joel McCrea in LONE HAND ('53), with Barbara Hale as the feminine lead.

Hunt's first role was a bit part in the Peter Lawford flick MY BROTHER TALKS TO HORSES ('46). Among his 33 credited appearances are small parts in THE FULLER BRUSH MAN ('48), starring "Red" Skelton and CHEAPER BY THE DOZEN ('50), with a cast that included Clifton Webb, Myrna Loy and Jeanne Crain. The film for which Jimmy gained the most acclaim was his role in INVADERS FROM MARS ('53), in which he shared top billing with Arthur Franz and Helena Carter. Hunt's final credit was in the 1986 remake of INVADERS FROM MARS where, no longer a child actor, he played the role of the "chief of police. The remake starred Karen Black and Hunter Carson.

Jimmy was born James Walter Hunt on December 4, 1939, in Los Angeles. His father, Walter "Win" Hunt was born in Montana and worked in the tool and die business. His mother, Hilda, a stay at home wife and mother, was born in Dayton, Ohio. His one sibling, a younger sister, Bonnie Lee Miller, now lives in San Diego County, and Jimmy says, "She was always supportive of me, and we were more best friends than brother and sister."

Jimmy graduated from Hamilton High School in Los Angeles and was a member of the school's football team. He then attended Santa Monica Community College for two years. He next spent three years in the army and was stationed in Germany where he worked as a decoder. It was during his tour of duty in Germany that he met his wife, Roswitha, a German native, who Jimmy says spoke no English when they met. The lack of communication was not an impediment as they entered into a marriage that has lasted nearly forty years. Asked if they married in Germany, Jimmy replied, "No, as that would have cost me my security clearance with the army."

Jimmy and Rowitha were wed on January 26, 1963, in Culver City, California. The couple has three children. A daughter, Rowitha, works as the "girl Friday" for author Jackie Collins. She is married, and has presented her parents with three grandchildren, two girls and a boy. Son Randy works for Prudential Life Insurance Company, is married, and is the father of two boys. Their final child, son Ron, works for Disney. He and his wife have four children, three girls and a boy. Think time doesn't fly? He is now a great-grandfather of three, courtesy of his son Ron.

Jimmy is now a sales manager for a Los Angeles tool supply firm. When asked about his hobbies and activities, he replied, "my church, my family, and sports." Jimmy's favorite screen role was in LONE HAND ('53), with Joel McCrea. He said of McCrea, "My favorite performer. A wonderful person who always treated me as a son." He is also a Glenn Ford fan. Jimmy and his wife reside in Simi Valley, California.

TEDDY INFUHR

Either actress Natalie Wood's mother was a paranoid, highly protective parent, or Teddy Infuhr was possessed with some very visible endearing and positive character traits, because the word out of Hollywood is that he was one of the few juvenile actors that Natalie's mother would allow her daughter to socialize with on the set.

Born Theodore Infuhr, the son of Frank and Rosalie Infuhr, in Saint Louis, Missouri, on November 9, 1936, Teddy was one of four children in the family. He reports he has two sisters and a brother, and his father was a chef and his mother a housewife.

The first of Teddy's 56 film roles was an un-credited appearance in PARDON MY SARONG ('42) with the comedy team of Abbott and Costello. During his twelve years before the camera that ended with MEN OF THE FIGHTING LADY ('54) with Van Johnson, Teddy had roles in the following films of note: MADAME CURIE ('43) with Greer Garson, SPELLBOUND ('45) with Ingrid Bergman and Gregory Peck, A TREE GROWS IN BROOKLYN ('45) with Dorothy McGuire, THE BEST YEARS OF OUR LIVES ('46) (a film that won numerous awards, starring Fredric March and Myrna Loy), THE EGG AND I ('47) with Fred MacMurray and Claudette Colbert, and DAVID AND BATHSHEBA ('51) with Gregory Peck and Susan Hayward. Included among this mix are three "Ma and Pa Kettle" movies.

Qualifying Teddy as one of the KID COWBOYS are his oaters with Charles Starrett in PHANTOM VALLEY ('48), WEST OF EL DORADO ('49) with Johnny Mack Brown, and three Gene Autry westerns, GENE AUTRY AND THE MOUNTIES, VALLEY OF FIRE, and HILLS OF UTAH, all ('51). Infuhr made three guest television appearances as a juvenile cowpoke with one "The Gene Autry Show" ('51) and two with "The Cisco Kid" ('52).

Teddy accomplished something no other "Kid Kowboy" did—he knocked out the hero. During a filming session while working in an Autry picture, Teddy was supposed to hit the bad guy over the head with the heavily padded bottom of an iron skillet. He swung and missed, hitting Gene instead with the unpadded side and Autry went "out like a light." Teddy says Gene was unconscious for only a few moments and wasn't too upset over the incident.

Teddy was educated at the Mother of Good Counsel School, Loyola High School and Loyola

University in Los Angeles, and later graduated from the Palmer College of Chiropractic Medicine in Davenport, Iowa. Capitalizing on the success he had with Natalie Wood's mother, he continues to rub people the right way as a practicing chiropractor. He also has taught at Cleveland Chiropractic College in Los Angeles.

Teddy's hobby is fishing. On July 20, 1963 he married Rita Cantini, and they have two sons, Todd and Tim. Infuhr was a member of the Army Reserves. He now resides in Thousand Oaks, California.

TOMMY IVO

Tommy Ivo made thirteen westerns as a "Kid Kowboy" during his stay in Hollywood.

Chatting with Tommy revealed him to be an interesting and personable individual who has lived life to its fullest. While most sources list Denver as the place of Tommy's birth, he says he was actually born in Littleton, Colorado, on April 18, 1936, and lived there until he was seven. Tommy's father, Hans Ivo, a meat cutter by trade, migrated from Germany at the age of one. His mother, Sara Paulsen, was a housewife of Danish descent. The family moved to Los Angeles in 1943 in search of a milder climate more conducive to Mrs. Ivo's arthritis. There was a brother, Don, who was seven years older than Tommy. Don joined the Marines and fought in Korea, but unfortunately, he lost his life in an automobile accident at age 24.

As a youngster, Tommy took tap dance lessons. Neither he nor his parents had any thoughts of an entertainment career for Tommy, but it was his tap-dancing ability that earned him his first film role in EARL CARROLL VANITIES ('45) with Dennis O'Keefe and Eve Arden as the leads.

Tommy says as a child he was frail, looked younger than his age, and was always the last one picked when sides were chosen for school games. Ironically, he went on to a career in sports that far surpassed any of his detractors. His education consisted of public schools in Burbank, California, graduating from Burrows High School and attending Glendale Junior College, but "for only nine days," he says.

Ivo's first western was SONG OF ARIZONA ('46) with Roy Rogers. Included among his other oater roles are six films in which he supported Charles Starrett: TRAIL TO LAREDO ('48), LARAMIE ('49), HORSEMEN OF THE SIERRAS ('49), TRAIL OF THE RUSTLERS ('50), SNAKE RIVER DESPERADOS ('51), and THE ROUGH, TOUGH WEST ('52). There are two westerns starring Gene Autry, HILLS OF UTAH and WHIRLWIND ('51), as well as SONG OF IDAHO ('48) with Kirby Grant, OUTCASTS OF THE TRAIL ('49) with Monte Hale, SMOKY MOUNTAIN MELODY ('48) with Roy Acuff and "Big Boy" Williams, and finally THE TREASURE OF LOST CANYON ('51) with an unlikely lead for a western, William Powell.

Tommy's guest roles in television included appearances on "The Gene Autry Show," "The Range Rider," "Adventures of Wild Bill Hickok," "The Adventures of Rin Tin Tin," "26 Men," "Leave it to Beaver," and "Petticoat Junction."

Lee Aaker played "Corporal Rusty" in all 165 episodes of "The Adventures of Rin Tin Tin," produced for television in the 1950s.

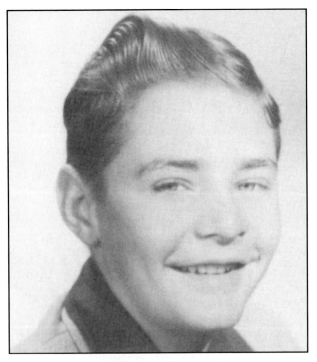

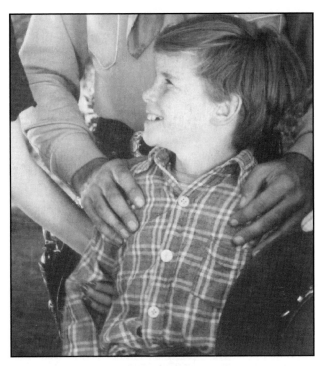

Studio portrait of Bobby Beers

Tommy Bupp

Gene Autry, Armida, and Ann Pendleton in ROOTIN' TOOTIN' RHYTHM (1937).

Michael Chapin

Wes Barry (third from left) had a good role in the Jack Randall western THE MEXICALI KID (1938). Also pictured: Ed Cassidy and Sherry Tansey.

Bennie Bartlett

Buzz Barton

Johnny Crawford with TV's Rifleman, Chuck Connors.

George Ernest

Tim Holt, briefly a KID KOWBOY, who went on to be a western star.

Bobby Blake, Milton Kibbee, and Ann Todd in a scene from the Allan Lane feature, HOMESTEADERS OF PARADISE VALLEY (1947).

Noah Beery, Jr.

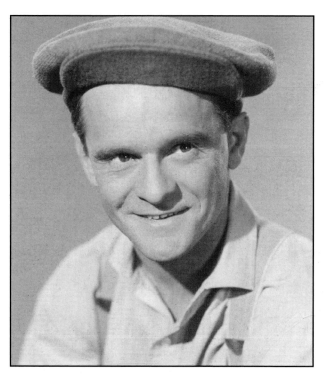

Sonny Bupp as he appeared in CITIZEN KANE (1941). The film's star, Orson Welles, selected Sonny for the role of his son because he saw a resemblance of himself in Sonny.

Frankie Darro

Jane Regan protects young Cope Borden as Robert Walker confronts Jack Perrin, who is restrained by Blackie Whiteford and Lew Meehan. Nelson McDowell is behind Meehan in this scene from TEXAS JACK (1935).

Junior Coghlan

Gene Autry smiles at the antics of Joe "Tadpole" Strauch, Jr. and Smiley "Frog" Burnette.

Tom Keene and Don Stewart together in WHERE TRAILS END (1942).

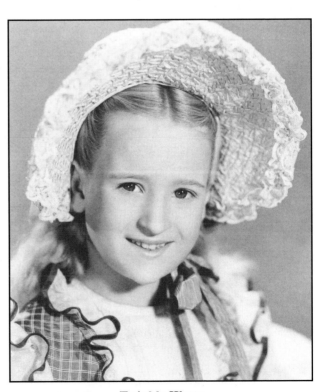

Twinkle Watts

Don "Red" Barry and Tommy Cook in THE ADVENTURES OF RED RYDER (1940).

Jane Withers   **"Rough Ridin'" Eilene Janssen**

Edith Fellows worked with Gene Autry in two 1942 movies, HEART OF THE RIO GRANDE and STARDUST ON THE SAGE. Also pictured is Louise Currie.

Johnny Duncan as "Robin" and Robert Lowery as "Batman"

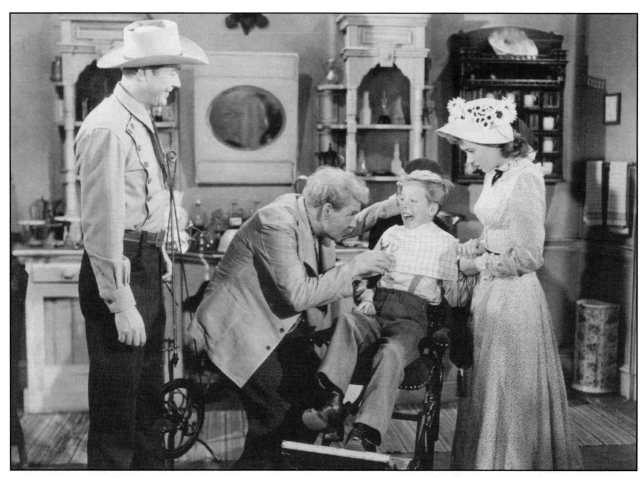

Tommy Ivo with Monte Hale, Paul Hurst, and Jeff Donnell in OUTCASTS OF THE TRAIL (1949).

Little Dick Jones with Jack Randall

Norma Jean Wooters is protected by Charles Starrett and Kay Harris in THE FIGHTING BUCKAROO (1943).

Gary Gray

Johnny Duncan is flanked by daughter Maranda and wife Susan at the 2002 Charlotte Film Festival.

Bobby Larson joins William Boyd in THE LEATHER BURNERS (1942).

Two of Hollywood's real "good guys": Kermit Maynard and Dick Jones in a scene from WILD HORSE ROUNDUP (1937).

Billy Gray with members of the cast of the hit television series "Father Knows Best." Front: Lauren Chapin and Billy Gray. Rear: Elinor Donahue, Robert Young, and Jane Waytt.

Harry McKim with Bill Elliott (who is holding a six-gun on LeRoy Mason) in a scene from MOJAVE FIREBRAND (1944).

Helen Parrish

Jimmy Rogers

Peter Miles in the Robert Mitchum film THE RED PONY (1949).

Paul Jordon with Don Barry & John Merton in a scene from BORDER RANGERS (1950).

Bruce Norman is being comforted by Allan "Rocky" Lane in a scene from SUNDOWN IN SANTA FE (1948). Also pictured: Russell Simpson and Rand Brooks.

Carol Nugent (center) with Allan Lane, Monte Hale, Penny Edwards, Gordon Jones and Roy Rogers in TRAIL OF ROBIN HOOD (1950).

Fred Sale, Jr. in a scene from WHEELS OF DESTINY (1934) with Ken Maynard and Frank Rice.

Eddy Waller, Duncan Richardson and Allan Lane in a scene from GUNMEN OF ABILENE (1950).

Tommy Ryan

Sammy McKim

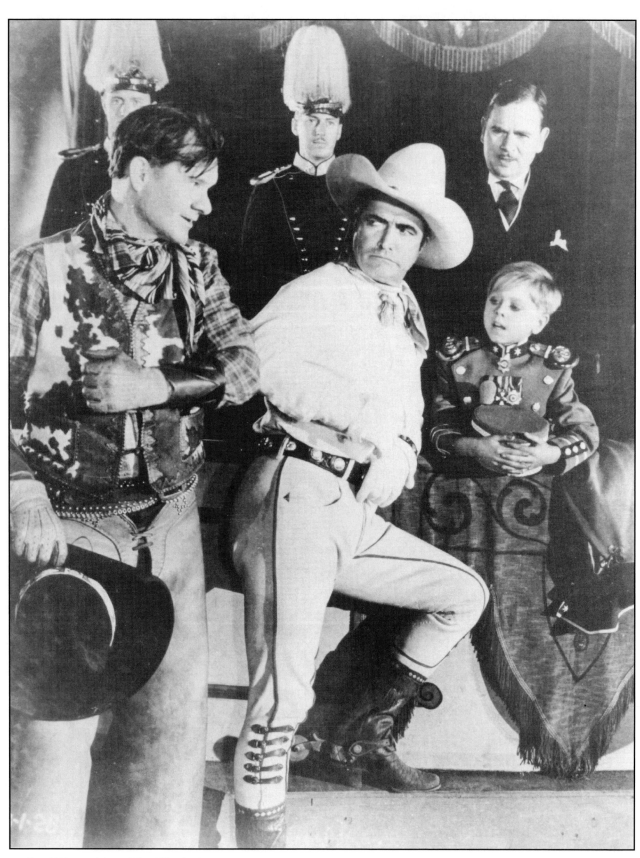

Paul Hurst, Tom Mix, Wallis Clark, and Mickey Rooney in a scene from MY PAL, THE KING (1932).

Dean Stockwell and Jeffrey Hunter talk as cast members Josephine Hutchinson and Janice Rule look on in this scene fom GUN FOR A COWARD (1957).

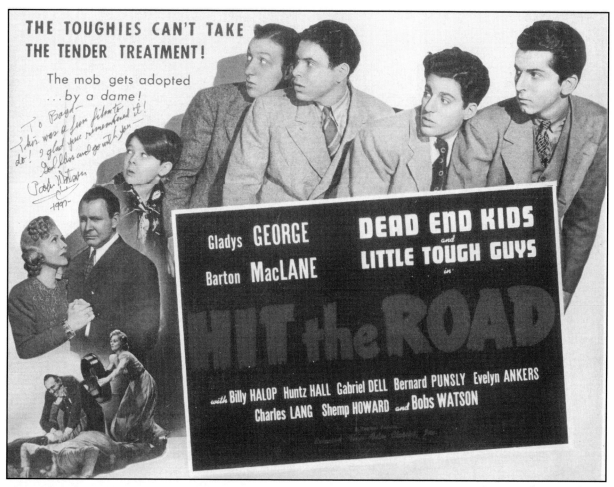

Bobs Watson (by his signature) in HIT THE ROAD (1941). Beside him are Huntz Hall, Bernard Punsley, Billy Halop, and Gabe Dell.

THROUGH THE YEARS

The publisher and author take great pride in presenting to you four very special couples. In the Hollywood community (as well as in other areas of the world) longtime marriages are a rarity. These four couples collectively have been married over 175 years. We congratulate them for this achievement. Without a doubt, they are among the nicest people in the world!

Gary and Jean Gray, married 42 years.

Sam and Dot McKim, married 48 years.

Dick and Betty Jones, married 55 years.

Harry and Julie McKim, married 30 years.

Ivo's non-westerns of note included parts in I REMEMBER MAMA ('48) with Irene Dunne, FATHER IS A BACHELOR ('50) with William Holden, and THE LEMON DROP KID ('51) with Bob Hope. Ivo's last credited role was in AMERICAN NITRO ('79) although he was un-credited for a stunt role in HEART LIKE A WHEEL ('83) where he doubled actress Bonnie Bedelia who was playing Shirley Muldowney, the pioneer female racing legend.

Tommy's true love was auto racing and he wanted to make it a second career. This resulted in him having to give up acting (as insurance companies refused to insure studios whose actors engaged in such a dangerous activity). His racing days were highly successful. Ivo held the world speed record in his class 11 different times. He was the first inductee into the National Hot Rod Association Hall of Fame; he was the recipient of an "Ollie," racing's equivalent of Hollywood's Oscar; he was presented with the industry's "Lifetime Achievement Award;" and the Bakersfield, California, track presents an annual award in Tommy's name.

There were downsides in those racing days—numerous wrecks, including a car engine exploding—that resulted in serious back, neck, and rib injuries. However, Tommy says his worst accident occurred at a Los Angeles track where his car was airborne, turned completely upside down and slid in that position for some distance with Tommy inside. He goes on to say, "I walked away without a scratch."

Tommy Ivo was a member of the California Air National Guard. At one time, Tommy was a partner in a Bekins moving van franchise. Tommy names Gary Gray and Dick Jones among his friends from his days as an actor. Tommy's present day interests and hobbies are flying, skydiving, scuba, and travel, including trips to Russia and China.

Tommy has been twice married, both times to Inez Andersen. They were first wed in 1971 and divorced five years later. The couple tried it again in 1982, and again called it quits after five years. There were no children. At present, Tommy has a lady friend, Sandy, whose company he has enjoyed for some 12 years.

His favorite screen role was THE LOST VOLCANO ('50) with Johnny Sheffield. His favorite actors include Boris Karloff, William Holden, William Powell, and Charles Starrett. Tommy calls the late Edmund O'Brien the most insensitive of all of the stars with whom he worked.

To close on a note of interest, Tommy says as a boy still living in Colorado, his favorite movie cowboy was Roy Rogers. He would spend time at a local theme park where he would ride the merry-go-round, always picking a horse that reminded him of "Trigger." Later in life he was able to purchase the merry-go-round "Trigger," and it now is part of the decor of his Burbank home.

EILENE JANSSEN

"The Rough Ridin' Kids," touted by Republic Pictures to be a junior version of the popular Roy Rogers-Dale Evans westerns, selected 11-year-old Eilene Janssen as the juvenile "Dale" to co-star with Michael Chapin in the series. The series made its debut in BUCKAROO SHERIFF OF TEXAS ('51) and endured through another three films: THE DAKOTA KID ('51), ARIZONA MAN-

HUNT ('51) and WILD HORSE AMBUSH ('52).

Eilene Janssen was born in Los Angeles on May 25, 1938. Her parents were Henry Karl and Mary Ellen Janssen. Her father worked for 47 years as a sound mixer for Universal Studios. Her mother was involved with opera. Eilene has no siblings. Her first claim to fame was as an infant when she won the Adhor Milk Baby contest. This resulted in her picture being displayed on the sides of milk trucks. The publicity from this award, and the fact her father was a studio employee, helped pave the way for her film career.

One of Eilene's grandfathers owned a dairy ranch, and at an early age she was riding horses. However, she says, the riding at her grandfather's ranch was not the riding required in the "Rough Ridin' Kids" series, so both she and Michael Chapin had to take lessons from noted riding master Ace Hudkins.

Part of Eilene's early education was (as was the case with most of the child players) at the studio school. She went on to graduate from Immaculate Heart High School and Immaculate Heart College. Among her early "suitors," she says, were Gary Gray and Tab Hunter, but hastens to add that Tab Hunter was only for publicity.

Eilene made her entry into films in SANDY GETS HER MAN ('40) when "Baby Sandy" (Sandra Lee Henville), the film's star, reportedly had an attack of "the vapors" and wouldn't perform, so Eilene stepped in. Her first credited role was in SINCE YOU WENT AWAY ('44), a film that starred Claudette Colbert, Jennifer Jones, and Shirley Temple. In addition to her roles in the "Rough Ridin' Kids" series, Janssen made two other juvenile appearances in westerns. She joined Jim Bannon in RENEGADES ('46) and was with William Boyd and Andy Clyde in BORROWED TROUBLE ('48). She also has an adult western to her credit as she co-starred with Brian Donlevy in ESCAPE FROM RED ROCK ('58).

Among Eilene's non-western film credits are roles in TWO GIRLS AND A SAILOR ('44) with Gloria DeHaven, June Allyson and Van Johnson, SONG OF LOVE ('47) with Katharine Hepburn, ON OUR MERRY WAY ('48) with Paulette Goddard and Jimmy Stewart, THE BRIDE GOES WILD ('48) with Van Johnson and June Allyson, THE BOY WITH GREEN HAIR ('48) with Pat O'Brien and Dean Stockwell, and THE SEARCH FOR BRIDEY MURPHY ('56) with Louis Hayward and Teresa Wright. She also had a role in PANIC IN THE CITY ('67) and then experienced a hiatus of thirty years before her final credit, MEANWHILE, BACK AT THE RANCH ('97).

Janssen's television appearances included roles in "Texaco Star Theater," "Sugarfoot," "The Rifleman," "The Gene Autry Show," "The Range Rider," "Tales of Wells Fargo," "The Beverly Hillbillies," "Perry Mason," and "Mister Ed."

Janssen also took singing, dancing, and marimba lessons as a youngster, and during the war she often was part of the troupe entertaining the servicemen. She says that she received citations from the U.S. Army, Navy, and Treasury for her USO work.

Eilene was the recipient of several other awards while still of tender years. She was the Ambassador Hotel's Miss Bathing Beauty in 1945, Little Miss America in 1946, winner of the Los Angeles Herald's Hollywood Bowl Better Babies Award. She was pictured on Weber's Bread for years as the Weber Bread Girl and was featured in ads for Challenge Butter, Dolly Madison cupcakes, and Heinz pickles.

As part of the publicity campaign for the "Rough Ridin' Kids" series, Eilene and Michael rode in the Pasadena Rose Bowl Parade, the Shriners Parade, and the Hollywood Christmas Parade.

Eilene was married on September 6, 1965, to George Moore, an attorney. The marriage produced five daughters: Jenny, Lisa, O'Erin, Mary, and Julie. George Moore passed away on August 26, 2000. It's hard to believe, but the "Rough Ridin' Kid" is seven times a grandmother. Eilene is busy these days settling up her late husband's law practice.

Eilene was an active lady. Her hobbies once included horseback riding, dancing, ice-skating, and tennis, but she says she has no time for them now. She is involved with the Pasadena Opera Guild, the Pasadena Symphony, and Los Angeles Opera Company. She can still be seen on an occasional commercial and says she is "not retired."

Her close friends in the industry are Gigi Perreau, Michael Chapin, Gary Gray, Margaret O'Brien, Mary Ellen Donahue, and Beverly Washburn.

Eilene's favorite roles were the three episodes on the "Texaco Star Theater," and her favorite performer is Donald O'Connor who starred with her on these shows.

AUSTEN JEWELL

Several sources, including information in his obituary, claim one-time juvenile actor Austen Jewell appeared in several Tom Mix westerns. A review of several film credit sources, and a check of the cast list of Mix's films confirms no such credits. (There was a Betty Jewell—whom Bill Russell, one of western films' better historians, feels may have been Austen's sister—who did make an appearance with Mix in MILE-A-MINUTE ROMEO ('23), but this relationship cannot be verified.) Austen Jewell is listed among the "Kid Kowboys" because he had a role with Buck Jones in BLOOD WILL TELL ('27). Other than his role in this western, Jewell has only four other film credits in the variety of sources checked: GREED ('25), WILD GEESE ('27), KING OF KINGS ('27), and CITY LIGHTS ('31).

Austen Jewell was born in Texas on November 17, 1915, the son of Stanley Jewell and Dagmar Nielsen. His father was born in Wisconsin and his mother in England. A well-educated man, Jewell was a graduate of U.C.L.A. After his college years, he served in the U.S. Navy in the Pacific Theater during World War II. Following the war, he returned to Hollywood where he served in many capacities in a career more distinguished than his days as a juvenile actor. He worked in a secretarial capacity to Harry Cohn at Columbia Pictures, put in several years with Disney, and later became self-employed in a few different motion picture facets.

As an assistant director Austen worked on many films, among them FRONTIER REVENGE ('48), BOMBA AND THE JUNGLE GIRL ('52), WICHITA ('55), KENTUCKY RIFLE ('56), CANYON RIVER ('56), FRIENDLY PERSUASION ('56), THE OKLAHOMAN ('57), GUNFIGHT

AT DODGE CITY ('59), INVITATION TO A GUNFIGHTER ('64), "Annie Oakley," television series ('54), and "Texas John Slaughter," the Disney television series ('58). As a production manager he was associated with several movie ventures including THE CINCINNATI KID ('65), THE WILD COUNTRY ('71) and the Oscar winning TERMS OF ENDEARMENT ('83). Jewell was director of "The Gale Storm Show," television series ('56) and the producer of the television series "Shane" ('56) with David Carradine.

Austen was married to Dorothy Heath, and their main place of residence was 1110 Manning Avenue, in Los Angeles, California. Jewell retired in 1993 and spent days each week on the golf course. He claimed his greatest achievement was a "hole in one."

Jewell passed away September 24, 1998, at age 82 at a second home at 1910 Vineyard, Vista, in San Diego County. He had been suffering from metastatic lymphoma for three months, but the immediate cause of his death listed as cardiopulmonary arrest of five minutes' duration. According to his obituary, Jewell was survived by his wife, two daughters: Nancy and Janet; three brothers: Stanley, Royce, and Hollis; and four grandchildren. Austen Jewell's remains were cremated and deposited in the ocean off the Los Angeles coast.

DICKIE JONES

In nearly all of the events and personalities that are part of our daily lives, we have a penchant for the answer to "who is number one?" So, in assessing the assortment of "Kid Kowboys" whose lives and careers are documented in this book—using such criteria as ability, talent, longevity, variety and quality of performances, awards and honors, relationship with fans, and style of life away from the camera—the answer as to who is "number one" among these players should become clear by reading on.

Richard P. Jones, Jr., was born on February 25, 1927, the only child of Richard Percy Jones, a newspaper operator, and Icie Teague Coppedge, a homemaker. He birthplace was Snyder, Texas, a small town just south of Abilene and west of Dallas. Dick relates, "I learned to ride about the same time as I took up walking." At the age of four he was already one of the attractions at local rodeos billed as the "world's youngest trick rider and trick roper."

Dick first gained the attention that led him to Hollywood while a five-year-old performing at the 1932 Texas State Fair. Cinema cowboy star Hoot Gibson, who possessed some riding and roping ability of his own, was the guest attraction at the fair and was impressed enough with Dick's ability and talent that he convinced Dickie's mother to bring him to Hollywood. A few days later, Mrs. Jones and the world's youngest professional cowboy arrived in "Tinsel Town," where they lived with "Skeeter" Bill Robbins and his wife Dorothy at Gibson's ranch in Saugus, California, until getting settled in their new environment. (Thus, with the possible exception of Buzz Barton, Dick had no peers among the "Kid Kowboys" when it came to the criteria of being able to perform as a true cowboy.)

In 1934 at the age of nine, Dick was at work on a film career that would include nearly 100 films and 200 television appearances that commenced with a stunt role in WONDER BAR ('34) starring Al Jolson, and finally ended with A BOY AND HIS DOG ('74) supporting Don Johnson and Jason Robards. During this interval there were starring roles and support roles in shorts, comedies, dramas, serials, and westerns. He worked with many of Hollywood's top stars and with most of the B-western heroes, but Dick says, "except for some odd reason, I never worked with my mentor, Hoot Gibson." (Thus, as to the criteria of longevity, Dick ranks among the high echelon.)

Dick's westerns as a "Kid Kowboy" include WESTWARD HO ('35) with John Wayne, MOON-LIGHT ON THE PRAIRIE ('35) with Dick Foran, DANIEL BOONE ('36) with George O'Brien, LAND BEYOND THE LAW ('36) with Dick Foran, WILD HORSE ROUNDUP ('37) with Kermit Maynard, RENFREW OF THE ROYAL MOUNTED ('37) with James Newill, SMOKE TREE RANGE ('37) with Buck Jones, HOLLYWOOD ROUNDUP ('37) with Buck Jones, BORDER WOLVES ('38) with Bob Baker, THE FRONTIERSMAN ('38) with William Boyd, LAND OF FIGHTING MEN ('38) with Jack Randall, and HI YO SILVER ('39) with Lee Powell. During these juvenile years there were also four "A" westerns for Dick including DESTRY RIDES AGAIN ('39) with Jimmy Stewart and Marlene Dietrich, BRIGHAM YOUNG FRONTIERSMAN ('40) with Tyrone Power and Linda Darnell, VIRGINIA CITY ('40) with Errol Flynn and THE OUT-LAW ('41) with Jane Russell.

Dick continued playing western roles as an adult, appearing in STRAWBERRY ROAN ('48) with Gene Autry, SONS OF NEW MEXICO ('50) with Autry, REDWOOD FOREST TRAIL ('50) with Rex Allen, ROCKY MOUNTAIN ('50) with Errol Flynn, FORT WORTH ('51) with Randolph Scott, WAGON TEAM ('52) , THE OLD WEST ('52), LAST OF THE PONY RIDERS ('53) all with Gene Autry, WILD DAKOTAS ('56) with Bill Williams, and REQUIEM FOR A GUN-FIGHTER ('65) with Rod Cameron and an all-star cast of "old time" cowboy greats including Johnny Mack Brown, Tim McCoy and Bob Steele.

Jones also had his share of serial roles. He joined Jack Mulhall and Frankie Darro in BURN 'EM UP BARNES ('34). This was followed by QUEEN OF THE JUNGLE ('35) with Reed Howes and Mary Kornman, CALL OF THE SAVAGE ('35) with Noah Beery, Jr. and Walter Miller, ADVEN-TURES OF FRANK MERRIWELL ('36) with Jean Rogers and Don Briggs, BLAKE OF SCOT-LAND YARD ('37) with Ralph Byrd and pretty Joan Barclay, and THE GREAT ADVENTURES OF WILD BILL HICKOK ('38) with Bill Elliott, Frankie Darro, Sammy McKim, and Kermit Maynard. He appeared as part of the "Our Gang" group on five occasions and was cast with Edgar Kennedy in a series of comedy shorts early in his Hollywood days. There were also roles in feature comedies where he supported the elite such as BABES IN TOYLAND ('34) with Laurel and Hardy, and KID MILLIONS ('34) with Eddie Cantor.

Jones had parts in numerous motion pictures with some of Hollywood's biggest names in pictures of "blockbuster" quality. Among this group were roles in NOW AND FOREVER ('34) with Carole Lombard, Gary Cooper, and Shirley Temple, LITTLE MEN ('34) with Ralph Morgan, WIFE VER-SUS SECRETARY ('35) with Jean Harlow, Jimmy Stewart, Myrna Loy and Clark Gable, BLACK LEGION ('36) with Humphrey Bogart, STELLA DALLAS ('37) with Barbara Stanwyck, YOUNG MISTER LINCOLN ('39) with Henry Fonda, MISTER SMITH GOES TO WASHINGTON ('39) with Jimmy Stewart. KNUTE ROCKNE, ALL AMERICAN ('40) with Ronald Reagan, VIRGINIA CITY ('40) with Errol Flynn, Randolph Scott and Humphrey Bogart, THIS GUN FOR HIRE ('41) with Alan Ladd and Veronica Lake, THE ADVENTURES OF MARK TWAIN ('43) with Frederic

March, HEAVEN CAN WAIT ('43) with Don Ameche and Gene Tierney, and SANDS OF IWO JIMA ('49) with John Wayne.

In 1940 Dick was the voice of "Pinocchio" in the Disney animated classic. He also appeared in many western television series as a guest performer on such shows as "The Lone Ranger," "The Gray Ghost" "Wagon Train," "The Gene Autry Show," and "Annie Oakley." Adding to all these accomplishments, Dick had lead roles in two popular television series: "The Range Rider" as co-star with Jock Mahoney, and "Buffalo Bill Jr.," and also in radio's "The Aldrich Family." (Put all of these successes together and they are unmatched in versatility, variety, and quality among the "Kid Kowboys").

In 1943 Dick and his mother traveled back east to New York City where he was to star in the popular weekly live radio show, "The Aldrich Family" in the role of "Henry Aldrich." Dick did not like New York City, so while his mother kept an apartment in the City, Dick lived and got his high school education at an up-state prep school. This meant commuting one day each week back to the "City" for his performance on the show.

This facet of his life was cut short upon receipt of a document stating, "Greetings." Proving his popularity wasn't limited to fans of the entertainment world, Dick, on June 8, 1945, received an invitation from Uncle Sam. He served a tour of duty in the U. S. Army during World War II as a rifleman in the infantry while stationed in Alaska. He was discharged on December 25, 1946, as a sergeant first class.

Back in Hollywood and not yet old enough to buy a beer, Dick took on a new role, that of a husband. On April 9, 1948, at the Hollywood Christian Church, Dick married his sweetheart, Betty Bacon. Betty is a California girl, a high school graduate with some college, and a stay–at–home wife, mother, grandmother, and great-grandmother. Dick Jones is among the few Hollywood stars who found that one wife was enough, but if one is lucky enough to be married to Betty Jones, why would he look elsewhere?

During their long marriage the Jones' clan has increased, but with no drop-off in talents and values. There were four children born to Betty and Dick: a daughter Melody, a son Richard III, and twins Jeffrey and Jennafer. Melody lives in Las Vegas and is the mother of two of Dick and Betty's grandchildren, Carolyn and Alexander. Dick relates that she also has five horses, three dogs, and many cats. Richard III, or Rick, lives in Medford, Oregon, and is the father of grandson Trevor. Jeffrey lives in Aliso Viejo, California, is the father of grandchildren Kyle, Kevin, and Kelsey. He is a dentist and a captain in the U.S. Army Reserves. Jennafer is a schoolteacher at a private Christian school in North Hollywood and lives in Northridge, California.

What about all these grandchildren? Carolyn is a marine biologist, and on August 24, 2001 she presented Dick and Betty with their first great-granddaughter, Savannah Rose. "About as big as a teacup," says the proud great-granddad. Alexander just completed Las Vegas High School and plans on becoming a programmer in computer design and animation. Kyle is an Eagle Scout, a varsity letterman in track and football at Aliso-Niguel High School, and he loves to fish. Kevin is a member of the junior varsity baseball and football teams at Aliso-Niguel High School. Kelsey is a student at Aliso-Niguel Middle School and is into diving and tumbling. Trevor, a whiz at computer games, is on a junior bowling team, plays the infield on a little league baseball team, and also loves fishing. The Jones clan is a close-knit, successful group with obvious positive family values.

Dick and Betty have attended several of the film festivals held annually across the country. They, together with Harry and Marilyn Carey, Gary and Jean Gray, and Peggy Stewart, are easily the most popular of the guest celebrities at these functions.

Some notes of possible interest in the life of Dick Jones:

• During his film career, when there was a break in the action, he did some radio work and participated in some rodeos. Following his active days in Hollywood, he worked in the real estate field as an appraiser and broker.

• Asked about his hobbies, Dick says, "fishing on the Rogue River (Oregon) with my kids, and around the San Juan Islands for salmon. And deep sea fishing, chasing the big tuna; I want to step up to a 300 pound one."

• How else is he spending his retirement years? "Just chasing fish and my grandkids."

• His favorite roles? "The part of 'Buck' in ROCKY MOUNTAIN ('50) and 'Dick West' in the 'Range Rider' television series with Jocko Mahoney."

• "In 1948 I dropped the "ie" from Dickie and became just Dick Jones."

• Dick's all-time favorite performer? "Errol Flynn."

Honors and recognitions Dick Jones has received:

• Dick was one of the original 1500 stars to be honored with a star on the Hollywood Walk of Fame for his contributions to the motion picture and television industries.

• In 1988 Jones was inducted into the Hollywood Stuntmen's Hall of Fame for outstanding stunt performances in motion pictures and television.

• In 1989 Dick received the prestigious Golden Boot Award from his peers in the western film world.

• In October 2000 Jones was the recipient of the Disney Legends Award at a ceremony at Walt Disney's Studio.

• Dick and Betty Jones reside in Northridge, California.

To answer the question posed early on as to the identity of the No. 1 "Kid Kowboy," without a doubt, it is Dick Jones.

BOBBY LARSON

Robert Boyd Larson was born in Los Angeles, California, on March 27, 1930. Among his over thirty film credits are six westerns, with five being appearances in "Kid Kowboy" roles, and one as a young adult. Larson made his screen debut in DOWN THE WYOMING TRAIL ('39) with "Tex" Ritter. His other oaters include RIDERS OF THE NORTHLAND ('42) with Charles Starrett, THE LEATHER BURNERS ('43) with William Boyd, ROBIN HOOD OF THE RANGE ('43) and SAGEBRUSH HEROES ('44) both with Charles Starrett, and REDWOOD FOREST TRAIL ('50) with Rex Allen.

Other notable films in which Bobby had roles include THE COURAGEOUS DR. CHRISTIAN ('40) with Jean Hersholt, THE BANK DICK ('40) with W. C. Fields, BACHELOR DADDY ('41) with Baby Sandy, HERE COMES MR. JORDAN ('41) with Robert Montgomery, HALF SHOT AT SUNRISE ('41) with Wheeler and Woolsey, WOMAN OF THE YEAR ('42) with Spencer Tracy, SHIP AHOY ('42) with Red Skelton, JACKASS MAIL ('42) with Wallace Beery, THE IRON MAJOR ('43) with Pat O'Brien, THE ADVENTURES OF MARK TWAIN ('44) with Fredric March, and THE SULLIVANS ('44) with Anne Baxter.

Larson appeared in three of the "Five Little Peppers" series with Edith Fellows: FIVE LITTLE PEPPERS AT HOME ('40), FIVE LITTLE PEPPERS IN TROUBLE ('40) and OUT WEST WITH THE PEPPERS ('40). He also made three appearances in the "Blondie" series, LIFE WITH BLONDIE ('45), BLONDIE'S LUCKY DAY ('46) and BLONDIE'S HOLIDAY ('47) with Penny Singleton and Arthur Lake.

Bobby was often featured on the "Lux Radio Theater." During the 1950s, Bobby served in the U. S. Navy during the Korean War. Following his acting career and his time in the service, he served as an elementary school teacher in Los Angeles from 1950 until his retirement in 1987.

Bobby Larson passed away on May 1, 2002, in Logan, Utah, a victim of Parkinson's disease.

BILLY LEE

Billy Lee, whose true name was William Lee Schlensker, was born on March 12, 1929, in the farming community of Nelson, Indiana (near the city of Terre Haute). Billy's parents, Pete Schlensker and Stella Hoskins, were both natives of Indiana. His father was a farmer. When Billy was three years old the family moved to California, reportedly because of Pete's asthmatic condition.

Once in California, Billy was enrolled at the Meglin School for Kiddies in Los Angeles. Ethel Meglin, the school's director, recognized Billy's early aptitude for song and dance, and soon Billy had his first film role in MIKE FRIGHT ('34), a "Little Rascals" short subject where he made an impressive debut with his tap dancing.

Billy's first feature film, and the first of six "Kid Kowboy" westerns, soon followed as he supported Randolph Scott in WAGON WHEELS ('34). His other western credits include roles in

ARIZONA MAHONEY ('36) with Buster Crabbe, THUNDER TRAIL ('37) with Gilbert Roland, IN OLD MONTEREY ('39) with Gene Autry, JEEPERS CREEPERS ('39) with the Weaver Brothers and Elviry, and Roy Rogers, and NEVADA CITY ('41) with Roy Rogers.

Among Billy's other films are starring roles in MAKE A WISH ('37) with Bobby Breen, SONS OF THE LEGION ('38) with Donald O'Connor, SUDDEN MONEY ('39), BOY TROUBLE ('39) with Charlie Ruggles and Donald O'Connor, THE BISCUIT EATER ('40) his most acclaimed role, REG'LAR FELLERS ('41) and WAR DOGS ('42). Lee's other films of note include SILK HAT KID ('35) with Lew Ayres, AND SUDDEN DEATH ('36) with Randolph Scott, THE BIG BROADCAST OF 1937 ('36) with Jack Benny, George Burns and Gracie Allen, COCOANUT GROVE ('38) with Fred MacMurray, LET US LIVE! ('39) with Henry Fonda, HOLD BACK THE DAWN ('41) with Charles Boyer, POWER DIVE ('41) with Richard Arlen, and MRS. WIGGS OF THE CABBAGE PATCH ('42) with Fay Bainter. Billy's final film was EYES OF THE UNDERWORLD ('43) with Richard Dix.

Billy's early school years were spent at the Paramount Studio school where his classmates included Bonita Granville and Billy Barty. He was the mascot of the studio's baseball team. Billy is credited with 12 years of education.

In 1943, with no explanation, Pete Schlensker took the family back to Indiana. Billy's father continued to book Billy for local vaudeville acts until Billy reached age 17. Billy then said, "enough," and left home. Of his father, Billy would later say, "Dad didn't like me quitting, but there was really nothing he could do about it. I don't know how much money I was paid or what happened to it. I do know that Dad never worked again after I went under contract, nor did he do anything after we returned to Indiana."

Billy next enlisted for a hitch in the U.S. Army. Right after he was discharged he was drafted, due to the Korean War. He spent the years 1951-1960 in the military. Fortunately, he was never in danger as both tours of duty were spent entertaining in officers' clubs as part of a musical combo.

Lee was married to Madeleine McBride. The couple had three daughters and a son and were blessed with seven grandchildren. Billy spent the last ten years of his life as a maintenance worker at a campground called Fisherman's Retreat, in Riverside County, California.

On November 17, 1989, at San Gorgonio Pass Memorial Hospital in Banning, California, Billy Lee passed away due to heart failure at age 60. Billy lies at rest at Riverside National Cemetery, 22495 Van Buren Boulevard, Riverside, California.

MARY LEE

Mary Lee, at age 13, was a featured singer with the Ted Weems dance band. In 1939, during a performance with the band in New York City, she was observed by Gene Autry and Republic Studios' head Herbert J. Yates, who encouraged her to come to Hollywood, where she would go on to play popular support roles in nine of Autry's westerns.

Mary Lee Wooters was born on October 24, 1924, in Centralia, Illinois, one of three daughters of Louis Wooters, a barber, and his wife, Lela. She was encouraged by her parents to pursue her obvious musical talent, which in turn led her to "Kid Kowboy" fame.

In the first of Mary's 20 Hollywood features she played the role of an obnoxious brat, in support of Bonita Granville, in NANCY DREW - REPORTER ('39). Over the next three years, while still under the age of 18, she appeared in the following Gene Autry oaters: SOUTH OF THE BORDER ('39), RANCHO GRANDE ('40), GAUCHO SERENADE ('40), CAROLINA MOON ('40), RIDE, TENDERFOOT, RIDE ('40), MELODY RANCH ('40), RIDIN' ON A RAINBOW ('41), BACK IN THE SADDLE ('41) and THE SINGING HILLS ('41). Mary's days in western films concluded in 1944 with roles in two Roy Rogers westerns, THE COWBOY AND THE SENORITA and SONG OF NEVADA. She is credited with appearing in a 1941 short, MEET ROY ROGERS, with a cast that included Rogers and Autry, as well as other cinema cowboys of note—Bill Elliott, Bob Baker, and Gabby Hayes.

Among Mary's several non-western films are credits in SING, DANCE, PLENTY HOT ('40) with Johnny Downs and Ruth Terry, BARNYARD FOLLIES ('40) with Rufe Davis, MELODY AND MOONLIGHT ('40) with Johnny Downs and Jane Frazee, ANGELS WITH BROKEN WINGS ('41) with Binnie Barnes and Gilbert Roland, SHANTYTOWN ('43) with John Archer, NOBODY'S DARLING ('43) with Louis Calhern and Gladys George, and THREE LITTLE SISTERS ('44) with Ruth Terry.

During Lee's brief career, she was on several radio shows, including an appearance with Edgar Bergen where she played "Priscilla Ramshackle," the girlfriend of Charlie McCarthy.

On November 12, 1943, at just 19 years of age, Mary secretly wed Sergeant Harry Banan. Following her final film, SONG OF NEVADA, with Roy Rogers, Mary retired to the Agoura Hills, California, where she worked with the Good Sam Club.

Sadly, on June 6, 1996, Mary Lee passed away at age 71. The cause of her death was not noted. Apparently, the marriage to Harold Banan was her only venture into wedlock, and there is no record she ever had children.

HARRY McKIM

The younger brother of Sammy McKim, Harry McKim was also a part of the group of juvenile players who supported those Hollywood heroes of the range. Harry says his credits listed on the Internet Movie Data Base are totally in error. As to his roles in oaters, he says, "I had a bit part IN OLD CALIFORNIA ('42) with John Wayne, a role with Don "Red" Barry in DAYS OF OLD CHEYENNE ('43), a good part in MOJAVE FIREBRAND ('44) with Bill Elliott, a high billing in NEVADA ('44) with Robert Mitchum, and a role in WANDERER OF THE WASTELAND ('45) with James Warren." Harry also appeared in the serial ADVENTURES OF RED RYDER ('40) with Don Barry and Tommy Cook.

As to his days in Hollywood, Harry said, "I actually started much earlier than the Data Base filmography states. I was working in motion pictures in 1935, at the age of five, the same year my brother Sam started. The whole family of five children started as extras through Central Casting at $5.50 per day, and we worked our way up from bit parts to roles in the movies. My earliest memories as a small child were working with my grandfather and brother Sam in some of the big scenes of SAN FRANCISCO ('36) with Clark Gable, Spencer Tracy and Jeanette MacDonald. I remember some special scenes in THE GREAT MAN VOTES ('39) with John Barrymore. My brother Sam and I were together in THE GREAT O'MALLEY ('36) with Pat O'Brien and Humphrey Bogart. Then I was in a few of the final "Our Gang" pictures. Some others that come to mind include bit parts in THE GREAT GILDERSLEEVE ('43), one of the "Henry Aldrich" pictures, THE HOUSE I LIVE IN ('46) with Frank Sinatra, and some special scenes with my sister Peggy and me playing war orphans from England in BABES ON BROADWAY ('41) with Judy Garland and Mickey Rooney." Harry went on, "I also recall a good part in HITLER'S CHILDREN ('42) with Tim Holt, and we were featured with pictures in *Life* magazine. In CIRCUMSTANTIAL EVIDENCE ('45) with Michael O'Shea and Lloyd Nolan, I had some good scenes with Nolan."

Harry's first and only marriage was on September 23, 1973, and he picked a winner. The new Mrs. McKim, Julie Moore, had been previously married and had two children, a son Jim and a daughter Lauri. Thus, Harry got to enjoy instant fatherhood without having to pace a hospital waiting room. The wedding took place at Portuguese Bend, California, a town located near San Pedro, in a beautiful all-glass chapel designed by the famed architect Frank Lloyd Wright, which overlooked the Pacific Ocean. Wife Julie's previous employment was as secretary to the vice-president of an Allstate Insurance Company office.

The author's first contact with the McKim family was with Julie, one of the more personal, pleasant, and vivacious ladies I have spoken to, as Harry was still at work. Yes, at age 72, Harry is still is busy at work. Asked why Harry wasn't thinking of retirement, Julie replied, "What would he do? He loves his work." Later conversations with Harry confirmed that his work is his hobby.

Tales of the McKim children and grandkids were related by Julie:

• Their son Jim and his wife Mary are both employed by Firemen's Fund Insurance—Mary as a customer account specialist, and Jim is a VIP underwriter. They both enjoy mountain biking, and their pride and joy, according to Harry, is a Westie named Lindsey. *(Not having a clue as to what a "Westie" was, I was enlightened by Julie that a "Westie" is a West Island Terrier, a dog.)*

• Daughter Lauri is married to contractor Bob Anderson, and she, too, is employed by Firemen's Fund Insurance as assistant associate to the vice-president. The couple has two children. Michael, who graduated in 2001 from the University of California at San Diego with a degree in political science and is now living in Washington, D.C. where he is an intern on the staff of Congresswoman Susan Davis by day, and having a grand time being a bartender by night. Daughter Katie, as was Michael, is a star soccer player and hurdler. Last year, at age 14, she was voted the outstanding female athlete at her middle school. She now attends Poway High School in San Diego County, the same high school brother Michael attended when he was voted the outstanding athlete in his senior year. It is obvious these grandchildren are the apples of Harry and Julie's eyes.

Harry was born in Seattle, Washington, on February 9, 1930. He graduated from North Hollywood

High School and spent two years at U.C.L.A. During World War II, Harry traveled with a large RKO cast performing stage plays over many of the western states, visiting Army and Air Force bases.

Harry served in the United States Army during 1948-49, and later became a member of both the Army Reserves and the California National Guard as a warrant officer. Today he is still working at the job he loves. He is a real estate developer and has built over 300 homes in southern California. Brother Sam says many of the homes in the area where Sam now lives were built by Harry, including Sam's half-acre view home.

Asked if he had a hobby, Harry replied, "Just what I do now—buying old homes which need extensive work, refurbish and remodel them, and put them back on the market." Harry has been elected the vice-president of the Woodlands La Jolla Association and the chairman of the association's architectural committee for 18 years. Nothing in this beautiful community where the McKims live happens or changes without Harry's stamp of approval.

Harry says his favorite feature film role was NEVADA. He tells of the following incident that occurred during filming: "My grandfather told us kids when a director or assistant director asks you if you can do something to tell them absolutely yes, whether you know how to do it or not." Harry was asked by a director if he knew how to drive a buckboard with two horses. He answered in the affirmative, even though he had never driven one, nor did he have any conception of how to go about the job. Filming commenced with Harry at the reins and Bob Mitchum in the back firing his gun at the bad guys who were close behind. The buckboard was totally out of control and both Harry and Mitchum bailed out.

Harry commented on some of the actors with whom he shared the silver screen:

• Don "Red" Barry, whom Harry supported in DAYS OF OLD CHEYENNE, was a constant user of filthy language in front of young kids.

• Scotty Beckett, who was part of the cast with Harry in CIRCUMSTANTIAL EVIDENCE, was a jerk. In a scene where the two were to engage in a boxing match in the ring, Beckett, at the urging of his mother, intentionally tried to rough Harry up. Beckett was older and larger than Harry. Beckett died on May 10, 1968, in Los Angeles, from a drug overdose.

• John Wayne was Harry's favorite. "A very friendly star. He took a great deal of time to help me in my small part. His children were often on the set and were extremely well behaved and courteous to everyone." Harry was with Wayne IN OLD CALIFORNIA.

The Harry McKims are one of Hollywood's class acts.

SAMMY McKIM

Sammy McKim, enjoyed by many for his screen roles, was also one to be admired for many other facets of his life. Born John Samuel McKim on December 20, 1924, in North Vancouver, British

Columbia, Canada, Sammy was the second of five children born to Walter and Lydia Edwards McKim. Sammy's dad was a lumberjack originally from Ontario who also worked as a furniture finisher. His mother was from Cardiff, Wales, and met Sammy's dad in British Columbia following World War I. Sammy had two brothers and two sisters, all of whom appeared in films at one time or another. The family moved to Seattle, Washington, when Sammy was starting school. This was during the "Great Depression," and Sammy's family, like many others, lost their home. This, coupled with Sammy's father's poor health, caused the family to move to California, first to the San Francisco area in 1934, and in the following year to Los Angeles. Sammy's father died in 1938, when Sammy was about fourteen, and his grandfather took over the role as head of the family.

Shortly after arriving in Los Angeles, Sammy and his grandfather, Harry Edwards, were visiting a cousin who worked at MGM. An MGM employee was impressed with the all-American boy look of the freckled-faced Sammy and sent him over to Central Casting with a letter of introduction. Shortly thereafter, Sammy was at work in the movies. Sammy's film career commenced with an un-credited role in 1935's, ANNIE OAKLEY. His final film appearance was a role in 1952's THUNDERBIRDS with John Barrymore, Jr., and Mona Freeman.

Lois Collier is sometimes referred to as the "fourth Mesquiteer," due to the many times she appeared with the western trio, "The Three Mesquiteers." Collier could share the title with Sammy because the majority of his "Kid Kowboy" roles were with this trio. Sammy McKim's western credits began in 1937 with the Mesquiteers trio of Bob Livingston, Ray Corrigan and Max Terhune in HIT THE SADDLE. Next, it was back with the same group in GUNSMOKE RANCH. Continuing in 1937, Sammy made the first of his three serial appearances with a role in THE PAINTED STALLION, in which he supported Ray Corrigan and Hoot Gibson and a cast that included former B-western stars Jack Perrin and Wally Wales. Also in 1937 Sammy had his third Mesquiteers role with a new threesome—Corrigan, Terhune, and Ralph Byrd—in TRIGGER TRIO. Next up, he joined Livingston, Corrigan and Terhune in HEART OF THE ROCKIES. His final 1937 western was with Charles Starrett in OLD WYOMING TRAIL. The year 1938 dawned with a role in Gene Autry's THE OLD BARN DANCE, followed by Sammy's second serial, THE LONE RANGER, with Lee Powell in the lead role. These were followed by roles in THE GREAT ADVENTURES OF WILD BILL HICKOK with Bill Elliott, his third serial role. Frankie Darro and Dickie Jones were other juvenile members of the cast, and Sammy's older brother David had a role as a bit-player. Two more Mesquiteers oaters followed: CALL THE MESQUITEERS, with Livingston, Corrigan and Terhune, and RED RIVER RANGE with John Wayne replacing Livingston.

In 1939 there were two more Mesquiteers westerns for Sammy: THE NIGHT RIDERS with Wayne again replacing Livingston, and NEW FRONTIER with Wayne, Corrigan, and now Raymond Hatton. The year 1938 closed out with Sammy teaming up with Charles Starrett in WESTERN CARA-VANS, and with Gene Autry in ROVIN' TUMBLEWEEDS. The year 1940 marked the end of the "Kid Kowboy" career for Sammy McKim when he made his last two western appearances. He was in his final Mesquiteers role in ROCKY MOUNTAIN RANGERS with the trio of Livingston, Duncan Renaldo and Raymond Hatton. McKim's last cowboy movie was with Don "Red" Barry in TEXAS TERROR. Over the next three years, Sammy had a few roles in some films of little consequence. Sammy relates that in the Charles Starrett film WESTERN CARAVANS ('39), in which he played the juvenile lead, that his younger brother Harry had a bit part.

During his years as a popular "Kid Kowboy," Sammy's image was used to endorse such products as Tootsie Roll, Daisy B. B. guns, Schwinn bicycles, and Mickey Mouse watches. Sammy says, "I did not get a nickel out of these endorsements. The studio made the profit."

One of Sammy's passions during his youth was art—sketching and drawing—a hobby that proved to be rewarding later in his life. McKim's early education was accomplished at the studio by teachers provided for the benefit of young players. He did graduate from Hollywood High School in the summer of 1942.

In April of 1943, during World War II, Sammy became a member of the U. S. Army. Author, Don Creacy, in an article on Sammy McKim published in *Cliffhanger* magazine, writes as follows: "...he was drafted into the U. S. Army in 1943. Sammy and his older brother had tried to volunteer in 1942 but had been turned down as they were not U. S. citizens." (Apparently, someone who is a citizen of a friendly country is subject to being drafted into the U. S. armed forces, but there are rules against non-citizens being allowed to volunteer for service.) Both brothers did, in fact, become members of the U.S. Army and served during World War II. Both became citizens while in the service.

Sammy entered basic training as an infantryman and was later sent to Los Angeles Community College for a course of a few months in the Army Specialized Training Program and then to the 89th Division. He then was sent to Officer Candidate School at Fort Benning, Georgia, and emerged as a 2nd lieutenant. Sammy was sent to the Philippines towards the war's end where he served briefly on Cebu and Luzon before being stationed in Japan as part of the occupation forces, joining the 11th Airborne Division. McKim was separated from the service on October 12, 1946, and returned to Hollywood. He then joined the Army Reserves as a 1st lieutenant in the infantry.

By this time, movie roles were not plentiful, so McKim went about furthering his already considerable art talent by enrolling in the Art Center School where he finished the normally four-year course in 32 months. He graduated with a Bachelor of Arts degree in advertising and illustration. Sammy, like many others, took advantage of the benefits of the G.I. Bill to further his education.

In September of 1950, on the day following his graduation, Sammy was called to duty again and in a short time found himself on assignment in Korea. He became a platoon leader in a rifle company and spent four and one-half months "on the line." He was next transferred to an Air Force unit where he served as an observer in T-6s marking targets for fighter air strikes. On his eleventh mission the pilot was wounded by ground fire, and the plane crash-landed. They were rescued by a "chopper." Sammy was credited with 82 combat missions with the Air Force unit. He later was company commander of the 8th Regimental Headquarters, 1st Cavalry Division for the remainder of his Korean duty. For his service during the Korean conflict, Sammy earned the Distinguished Service Cross, a Bronze Star, 2 air medals, and various other military awards.

Work before the camera was again slow upon McKim's return to Hollywood. He then continued his art education, using the G.I. Bill, at the Chouinard Art Institute in Los Angeles. Next he went to work for 20th Century Fox in the studio art department as an illustrator. Upon leaving Fox, Sammy went to work with Disney Studios for the next thirty-two years before retiring in January 1987. Retirement gave Sammy time to pursue another of his hobbies—fishing.

In addition to his many art projects and exhibitions for Disney, Sammy managed to find time to teach art for ten years at the Art Center College of Design in Pasadena, California. His art is part of the collections housed at the U. S. Air Force, Los Angeles County Sheriff Department, and the Mormon Church, as well as private collections.

Some notes and comments of interest on the life and times of Sammy McKim:

• His mother: "Mother was an outstanding home-maker, raising five kids."

• His siblings: "David was 2 years older than I, Lydia, two years younger, Harry, five years younger, and Peggy, seven years younger. We all worked in films. I was the first in the movies (summer of 1935) in Jane Withers' film, THIS IS THE LIFE. I was an extra. David and Lydia both passed away during 1993."

• Hobbies and Activities: "Nothing much except art. We traveled a lot, four times to Scotland."

• Marriages: "Only one! Married Dorothy Hayes on March 12, 1955. That was the best thing I ever did. We have two sons, both artists. Brian, 45, is an animator with Disney Feature Animation. Matt, 39, was a model builder and project designer for 13 years at Walt Disney Imagineering and is now free-lancing."

"My older brother David married Virginia Hayes in 1952. I saw that David didn't have any mother-in-law trouble, so I proposed to Virginia's younger sister, Dorothy, and married Dot in 1955. (a family joke)."

"Brian has been married to another Dorothy since April '89, and they have given us 2 grandkids. Tyler will soon be ten and loves to draw and paint—another artist coming up. Natalie is a sweet and lovely little six-year-old. My Dot and I certainly enjoy these kids. Brian and Matt are great guys, and we see them and the grandkids regularly."

• His Disney Days: "I did the first Disneyland souvenir map which is famous among Disneyana collectors and fans. I also drew the first souvenir map for Disneyland Paris. They brought me out of retirement for that one, and I understand they're still using it."

"Four or five years ago my name was added to the list of 'Disney Legends,' with special ceremonies, a heavy bronze trophy with engravings, signatures and hand prints in cement. Roy E. Disney, Walt's nephew, along with Michael Eisner, chairman and CEO, made the presentations with Mickey, Minnie, Goofy, Donald, and other characters joining in along with the Disneyland band."

"I made production art work for the Lincoln attraction sponsored by the state of Illinois for the '64-'65 New York World's Fair. When Walt brought 'Great Moments With Mr. Lincoln' to Disneyland in '65, I did all the pre-show paintings of the life of Lincoln, 34-35 of them projected on an 8 x 28 inch wide screen—before the audience went inside to the sit-down theater to see and listen to the audio-animatronic figure of our 16th president."

• His favorite performers: "All the cowboy actors I worked with."

• His favorite screen role: "Young Kit Carson in the 1937 Republic 12 chapter serial, PAINTED

STALLION."

• His retirement years: "I enjoy travel with my family, take lots of vacation photos, do some freelance art work, and am active with our church."

Sammy and Dot McKim reside in Sunland, California.

In all aspects of life, Sam McKim is a winner.

FREDDIE MERCER

Reading RKO's early press releases on juvenile actor Freddie Mercer, one had to believe he was reading about the next Sir Laurence Olivier. Such was not the case. Freddie Mercer was born Freddie Musser March 6, 1929, in Detroit, Michigan, the son of Dr. and Mrs. Fred C. Musser.

RKO first advises us: "Possessing one of the finest boy soprano voices in the West, and gifted with unusual acting talent, Freddie Mercer is one of the few child actors in Hollywood who seems definitely slated to continue his career successfully." The studio goes on to let us know: "In addition to inheriting musical talent from his mother, who was a church soloist before her marriage, Freddie has been taking voice lessons since he was six years old. Under the tutelage of Prof. Harry Seitz, the boy advanced so rapidly that he became the soloist of the Detroit Symphony at the age of nine; also soloist in St. Paul's Cathedral. He sang frequently over Radio WXYZ in Detroit, likewise in New York on various NBC programs."

In the late 1930s, when Freddie first arrived in Hollywood, RKO announced: "Freddie came to Hollywood to sing at the National Music Conference. Helene Tardival Byers, noted New York concert pianist and at that time one of the sponsors of the Turnabout Theater in Hollywood, heard the youngster and sent for him to star in a circus show at that playhouse. His first performance was seen by director Harold Schuster, who promptly signed Freddie for the second lead with Roddy McDowell in 20th Century Fox's ON THE SUNNY SIDE ('42). In the opinion of many preview critics, the unknown boy 'stole' the picture." Further from RKO, "Shortly after ON THE SUNNY SIDE was completed, Freddie played the part of "young Poe" in THE LOVES OF EDGAR ALLAN POE ('42). He next appeared with Ginger Rogers in THE MAJOR AND THE MINOR ('42)."

Press releases continue: "Then RKO Radio stepped in and signed Freddie to a long-term contract. The youngster was just the type needed for the important role of Leroy in THE GREAT GILDERSLEEVE ('42), Harold Peary's first RKO Radio starring vehicle. Freddie also played the same part in the second of this series, GILDERSLEEVE'S BAD DAY ('43)." More from RKO: "Although Freddie sang only once in his first five pictures, warbling an aria from the opera "Martha" in THE GREAT GILDERSLEEVE, the beauty of his voice is attested by the constant request for his appearance at public functions. He has sung at the Hollywood Bowl, at the Tournament of Roses in Pasadena, before the League for Crippled Children, and at the ball given by officers and cadets at the Ambassador Hotel." And, "Aside from his singing, Freddie's hobby is photography. He has his own dark-room, and he develops and prints all his pictures."

Now, back to reality... Mercer's Hollywood film career spanned the years 1940-1944. His first two films, FIVE LITTLE PEPPERS IN TROUBLE in 1940 and THE MAJOR AND THE MINOR in 1942 were both un-credited roles. His third film gains him membership as a "Kid Kowboy" as he appeared in the 1942 "Three Mesquiteers" oater, SHADOWS ON THE SAGE, in which he follows paranoid sheriff Harry Holman around, sneaking up on Holman so that Harry can practice his "quick draw." ON THE SUNNY SIDE, THE LOVES OF EDGAR ALLAN POE, and the first of his four appearances in GILDERSLEEVE films were also 1942 releases. The year 1943 saw him in two additional GILDERSLEEVE movies. In 1944 he made an appearance in a Bob Crosby musical, MY GAL LOVES MUSIC, and in the final "Gildersleeve" movie. That was it—the end of RKO's claim of greatness.

David K. Bowman, in a mini-biography, writes of Mercer, "His promising career ended abruptly in 1944 for unknown reasons."

PETER MILES

If but a portion of the researched information on the life of "Kid Kowboy" Peter Miles is correct and not Hollywood hype, he led a most eventful life. It is easy to verify Peter's roles as a juvenile actor in western films. He made support appearances in HEAVEN ONLY KNOWS, reissued as MONTANA MIKE ('47) with Robert Cummings, THE RED PONY ('48) with Robert Mitchum, TRIGGER, JR. ('50) with Roy Rogers, and CALIFORNIA PASSAGE ('50) with Forrest Tucker.

Peter was born in Tokyo, on April 1, 1937, according to information released by MGM. Peter's father was a French national engaged in banking and securities and was living in Japan conducting business when Peter was born. His mother was an American citizen born in Brooklyn, New York.

The following are portions of three separate press releases:

> "Pete was born in Tokyo where his father was in business selling stocks and bonds. The threesome escaped the Sine-Jap war and went to Paris as the father was a French national. But the holocaust pursued them and Papa joined the French forces in 1939 when his son was only a few months old. During the Nazi invasion of France the family was broken up, with Pete and his mother caught behind the enemy lines. Eventually they were all reunited in Paris where Nazi officers boarded in their house and soldiers slept in the stables. Yet the family managed to work with the underground. With forged passports, Pete and his parents escaped to Spain en route to Portugal. Later the family boarded a freighter in Lisbon."

> "...the war did occur, and with his French father and American mother, the future actor fled from France in late 1940 to join his maternal grandparents in Los Angeles."

> "His earliest recollections are of Nazi-occupied Paris. When France surrendered, his father and three uncles joined the underground. As an American neutral, his mother was free to leave France. As a woman, she was love bound to remain with

her husband. In 1940 the underground activities of two of his uncles caused their arrest and confinement in a concentration camp. Peter's father knew that his own arrest was near and inevitable. His value to the underground was ended. Pete was two years old, and his mother was large with her second child. It was 200 miles to the Portuguese border. His parents set out for the border on foot—his father carrying him in a basket. Aided along the way by Resistance members, dodging the Gestapo all the way, the family reached and crossed the border less than an hour before it was closed by the Nazis. Having walked the more than 200 miles in four days, they reached Lisbon just in time to board the last boat to leave that port for America."

(Does a man carrying a three and one-half year old boy in a basket and a woman pregnant into her third trimester walking over 200 miles in four days strain your imagination?)

Another point of concern: By all accounts the family reached Los Angeles in late 1940 or early 1941. However, the Internet Movie Data Base credits Peter with roles in MURDER WILL OUT and JUST WILLIAM, both 1939 films.

Contained in the aforementioned press releases are several versions of how Peter gained entry into films:

One has Peter's mother visiting MGM to audition Peter's younger sister for a role. The sister obtained the role, and later on the studio also offered a role to Peter.

Another version has Peter and his mother walking in the rain and being splashed by the car of a motorist. The motorist, who turned out to be a prominent actor's agent, stopped to apologize, and was so taken by Peter that he urged the mother to let him enter films. The mother was not interested, but after the persistent agent continued to make several more contacts, the mother agreed.

Then there is this story:

"It was purely because he was bi-lingual that Peter became the first actor in the family. Michael Curtiz was desperate. He had to find a five-year-old boy who could speak French to portray the son of Humphrey Bogart and Michele Morgan in his picture PASSAGE TO MARSEILLES ('44). A girl working in the studio office knew Peter's mother and suggested she take Peter to the studio. She complied, and Peter was signed for the role."

Take your pick.

Peter's other film credits include roles in ABBOTT AND COSTELLO IN HOLLYWOOD ('45), ENCHANTMENT ('48) with David Niven and Teresa Wright, THE RED PONY ('48) with Robert Mitchum and Myrna Loy, a film in which director Lewis Milestone gave him the screen name Peter Miles, ROSEANNA McCOY ('49) with Farley Granger and Charles Bickford, a film that earned him The New York Times Award, and QUO VADIS? ('51) with Robert Taylor and Deborah Kerr. Peter Miles' final juvenile role was supporting Cornell Wilde and Maureen O'Hara in AT SWORD'S POINT ('52).

Miles made television guest appearances on "Perry Mason," "Alcoa Presents," and "Maverick." He retired as a juvenile actor in his early teens.

Peter's education was extensive and impressive. He completed his elementary education at the Hal Roach and MGM studio schools and graduated from Loyola High School in Los Angeles. Reportedly, Peter then spent two years at Georgetown University in Washington, D.C., took classes at the University of Fribourg in Switzerland and at The Sorbonne in Paris. He then spent time traveling through France, Switzerland, Italy, Austria, the Scandinavian countries, Spain and Portugal, before returning to America to enroll at U.C.L.A. to pursue master's and doctorate degrees. A couple of events preceded and interrupted his education at U.C.L.A: First he legally changed his name to Richard Miles; and secondly, he accepted a role in the 1959 television series, "The Betty Hutton Show."

Miles' given name was Gerald Perreau-Saussine, and he is the brother of actresses Gigi and Janine Perreau. One studio commenting on the family background states: "Peter's mother Eleanor is American. His father Robert, a banker and importer, is French. His paternal grandfather was honorary dean of the Paris Stock Exchange. Further up on the family tree are the names of the Marquis de Saussine, Count Perreau, and those of various lieutenants of William the Conqueror. He is also connected genealogically to Charles Perreau who authored *The Sleeping Beauty* and *Cinderella* and to Claude Perreau who designed a section of The Louvre."

Peter and sister Gigi appeared together several times on the silver screen. Among the films are ENCHANTMENT ('48), ROSEANNA McCOY ('49), SONG OF SURRENDER ('49) with Wanda Hendrix and Claude Rains, YOLANDA AND THE THIEF ('45) with Fred Astaire, and FAMILY HONEYMOON ('48) with Claudette Colbert and Fred MacMurray. They also were both part of the cast on television's "The Betty Hutton Show."

This former "Kid Kowboy" was also an author. While a student at U.C.L.A. Miles was the winner for two consecutive years of the $2,000 Samuel Goldwyn Creative Writing Award for his novels *The Moonbathers* and *Angel Loves Nobody*. He is also the author of *That Cold Day in the Park*, and *They Saved Hitler's Brain*.

What else happened in the life of Peter Miles? Relying on information provided by Miles, the studios, and various media sources, we are told:

• Miles was a talented painter who had some of his oils displayed in Los Angeles galleries.

• He was an amateur magician.

• He was a member of his high school tennis team.

• At Georgetown University he was a member of the tennis team, art editor of the Georgetown Journal, and a member of the debate team.

• He was winner of three state junior tennis titles.

• He had poetry published in magazines in both the United States and Europe.

• He dated a lot and likes girls, but never married.

• He enjoyed sports and participated in not only tennis, but also skiing, ice skating, swimming, and horseback riding.

• He spoke Italian, German, French, and English.

• As a spectator, he enjoyed bull fighting and horse racing.

• His favorite vacation spot was the Costa Brava in Spain.

• His favorite writers were Carson McCullars, Salinger, Hemingway, Maugham, and Aldous Huxley.

• He considered *The Bible*, *Ulysses*, *Anna Karenina*, and *Madame Bovary* the greatest books ever written.

• His loves were grand opera, French and Lebanese cooking, walking in the rain, listening to records in the dark while sitting on the floor, and collecting first editions, antique guns, and old and new recordings.

• He was frugal. He saved S & H Green Stamps and was extravagant in that he drove an Austin-Healy Le Mans.

• He was a big movie fan and considered Rudolph Valentino and Greta Garbo the greatest of the legendary actors. Of later date players he favored Montgomery Clift, Dorothy Malone, and his sister Gigi.

Peter spent many of his final years living in Honolulu. Sadly, Peter Miles passed away as a cancer victim on August 3, 2002, in Los Angeles.

TERRY MILES

An obscure obituary notice in the *Los Angeles Times* of September 1, 1993, stated that Miles was a child actor in westerns and "Our Gang" comedies. However, a search of the *American Film Institute Catalog of Feature Films* and the supposedly complete cast list for "Our Gang" players in *Child and Youth Actors, Filmographies of their Entire Careers, 1914-1985*, by David Dye revealed no Terry Miles credits in either western films or "Our Gang" comedies.

In browsing through author Buck Rainey's book *Heroes of the Range,* there is a reproduction of a movie still from the western film WALLOPING WALLACE ('24) with Buddy Roosevelt, Violet LaPlant, and a juvenile player named Terry Myles, pictured. Terry Myles and Terry Miles were one and the same, and the only film credit for the young Miles was in the Buddy Roosevelt western. Terry Miles was the actor's true name, but for some reason, the spelling "Myles" was used in what appears to be his only film appearance.

Terry was born in California on February 24, 1919, and was credited with 12 years of education. Terry's father was Norbert A. Miles, born in West Virginia in 1887. Norbert was active in Hollywood, credited as a writer, director, and actor. His first writing credit was for THE DAUGHTERS OF DAWN ('20), a film that he is also credited with directing. His acting career ran from 1915, with a role in THE WIDOW'S SECRET, to 1933 when he appeared in SECRETS OF HOLLYWOOD. Norbert, too, used the spelling Myles as his professional surname, as Norbert A. Myles was credited as the scenario writer for the Roosevelt film in which Terry appeared. Terry's mother was Ethel B. Phillips, who was born in France.

During World War II, Terry served from 1941-1945 with the U.S. Army's 57th Signal Battalion, seeing service in North Africa, Italy, France, and Germany. Later, using his true name, he served for many years as a self-employed Hollywood make-up artist. Among his credits as a make-up artist is the film BLAZING SADDLES ('74).

Miles was married to Irene Kniss, a marriage that endured for 47 years and produced a son Nelson, two daughters, Brooke and Kathleen, six grandchildren, and one great-grandchild. Terry and his wife made their home at 1806 Stanford Avenue, Redondo Beach, California.

Terry Miles passed away at the Good Samaritan Hospital in Los Angeles on August 28, 1993. He had had surgery two days earlier. The causes of his death were stated to be small cell cancer, cerebral muscular disease, and hypertension. His remains were cremated and given to the family residence.

BOBBY NELSON

Bobby Nelson was one of the most prolific of the "Kid Kowboys" in terms of the number of westerns in which he appeared and the many different B-western stars that he supported.

Bobby Nelson's career in films commenced with a supporting role to cowboy star Bob Custer in THE FIGHTING BOOB ('26). Thus began a nearly twenty-year span of films that ran the gamut from short subjects, westerns, serials, and jungle movies.

From 1926 through 1928, Bobby kept busy with roles in BORDER WHIRLWIND ('26) again with Bob Custer, BULLDOG PLUCK ('27) still with Bob Custer, PERILS OF THE JUNGLE ('27) a serial with Eugenia Gilbert and Frank Merrill, and a second serial, TARZAN THE MIGHTY ('28) starring Merrill and Natalie Kingston. Over the next two years Bobby starred as "The Pioneer Kid," in a series of what appears to be western short subjects. The series included DANGEROUS DAYS ('29), WAIF OF THE WILDERNESS ('29), THE KID COMES THROUGH ('29), BOY AND THE BADMAN ('29), ORPHANS OF THE WAGON TRAIL ('29), THE POST OF HONOR ('30), ALIAS THE BANDIT ('30), THE BATTLING KID ('30), THE DANGER CLAIM ('30) and THE LAST STAND ('30).

Following "The Pioneer Kid" series, Bobby went back to supporting roles in features and serials. His credits over the next 15 years included ROARING RANCH ('30), with Hoot Gibson, HEROES OF THE FLAMES ('31), another serial starring Tim McCoy, TWO-FISTED JUSTICE ('31), with Tom Tyler, SPELL OF THE CIRCUS ('31), a serial with Francis X. Bushman Jr. and Alberta Vaughn, BATTLING WITH BUFFALO BILL ('31), another serial with Tom Tyler and Rex Bell, TWO GUN CABALLERO ('31) with Robert Frazer, PARTNERS ('32), with Tom Keene, DARING DANGER ('32), with Tim McCoy, COWBOY COUNSELLOR ('32), with Hoot Gibson, THE TEXAN ('32), with Buffalo Bill Jr., KING OF THE ARENA ('33), with Ken Maynard, THE WAY OF THE WEST ('34), with Wally Wales, TEXAS TERROR ('35), with John Wayne, CYCLONE OF THE SADDLE ('35), with Rex Lease, COWBOY AND THE BANDIT ('35), with Rex Lease, THE THROWBACK ('35), with Buck Jones, ROUGH RIDING RANGER ('35), again with Lease, THE GHOST RIDER ('35), with Johnny Mack Brown, THUNDERBOLT ('36), with Kane Richmond, VALLEY OF THE LAWLESS ('36), back with Johnny Mack Brown, CUSTER'S LAST STAND ('36), a serial with Rex Lease and William Farnum, THE GAMBLING TERROR ('37), with Johnny Mack Brown, GUN LORDS OF STIRRUP BASIN ('37), with Bob Steele, THE RED ROPE ('37), with Bob Steele, and BOOTHILL BRIGADE ('37), Johnny Mack Brown.

Many of the films in which Bobby Nelson appeared, including the entire "Pioneer Kid" series were directed by Jack T. Nelson, one of the busiest directors during western films' glamour years. Nelson had a long career in western films—both as an actor and as a director—commencing as early as 1914. He was born in Memphis, Tennessee, on October 15, 1882, and passed away on November 10, 1948, at North Bay, Ontario, Canada. Due to having the same surname, and the fact that Jack T. Nelson was so involved in Bobby's films, it has been widely assumed that the relationship was that of father and son. Apparently, this was not the case.

Robert John Nelson was born on July 21, 1923, in Santa Monica, California. Bobby was the son of David John Nelson, who was born in Kansas, and Barbara Easton, born in Scotland. Nelson's film career apparently ended with the Johnny Mack Brown western, BOOTHILL BRIGADE in 1937. After graduation from high school, Bobby served his country from 1943 to 1945. He was a college graduate and worked for 43 years as a self-employed certified public accountant.

Bobby was married to Helen Tidball, and the couple resided at 922 Freeman Street, in Santa Ana, California. It could not be ascertained whether the Nelsons had children.

On August 5, 1993, Bobby Nelson died at St. Joseph Hospital in Orange, California, at the age of 70 from gastric carcinoma, a malady from which he had suffered for the final five months of his life. Bobby's wife, Helen, was among his survivors. Today, Bobby Nelson lies at rest in Fairhaven Memorial Park, 1702 Fairhaven Avenue in Santa Ana.

CAROL NUGENT

Carol Nugent, the sister of "Kid Kowboy" Judy Nugent, was also a juvenile player in western films. Carol had roles in TRAIL OF ROBIN HOOD ('50) with Roy Rogers, THE STORY OF WILL ROGERS ('52) with Will Rogers, Jr. and Jane Wyman, and in THE LUSTY MEN ('52) with Robert Mitchum and Susan Hayward.

Among the non-western films in which she appeared are SECRET COMMAND ('44) with Pat

O'Brien, LITTLE MISTER JIM ('46) with "Butch" Jenkins, THE SEA OF GRASS ('47) with Spencer Tracy and Katharine Hepburn, IT HAD TO BE YOU ('47) with Ginger Rogers, GREEN DOLPHIN STREET ('47) with Lana Turner, and VICE RAID ('59) with Mamie Van Doren.

Carol's guest roles on television included appearances on "Death Valley Days," "Adventures of Wild Bill Hickok," "Perry Mason," "The Rebel," and "Family Affair."

Carol's birth information remains a Nugent family secret. According to her sister Judy, Carol was a "Kid Kowboy" who was afraid of horses.

Carol was married to actor Nick Adams, and the couple had two children. Unfortunately, the marriage came to an end in 1968 when Adams allegedly took his own life by a drug overdose.

Carol lives in Montana, just a few miles from the ranch run by her sister Judy. After being widowed for over thirty years, the word is that Carol is about to remarry. We wish her well.

JUDY NUGENT

In real life, Judy Nugent is about as close to being a "real cowboy" as one can get—she operates her Coyote Canyon Ranch in Ennis, Montana.

Judy Ann Nugent was born in Los Angeles on August 22, but the year was not disclosed as is a woman's prerogative. However, I am certain that the 1947 date used by writer Harris M. Lentz, III in his book, *Western and Frontier Films and Television Credits,* is incorrect, inasmuch as Judy was in her first film some four years earlier. In an interview with writer Mike Fitzgerald for *Western Clippings*, Judy related that her father was a prop man for MGM and that he had pictures of both Judy and her sister Carol on the sides of his prop box. This resulted in both girls being offered roles in THE MAN FROM DOWN UNDER ('43) with Charles Laughton when Judy was barely out of diapers. Judy's sister Carol is the older of the two Nugent girls, and is also one of the "Kid Kowboys."

As a juvenile, Judy's western film credits include NIGHT STAGE TO GALVESTON ('52) with Gene Autry, and DOWN LAREDO WAY ('53) with Rex Allen. Some of her non-western credits include roles in IT HAD TO BE YOU ('47) with Ginger Rogers and Cornel Wilde, CITY ACROSS THE RIVER ('49) with Stephen McNally, MAGNIFICENT OBSESSION ('54) with Jane Wyman and Rock Hudson, MA AND PA KETTLE AT HOME ('54) (sister Carol was also part of the cast), NAVY WIFE ('56) with Ralph Bellamy and Claire Trevor, THERE'S ALWAYS TOMORROW ('56) with Barbara Stanwyck and Fred MacMurray and THE GIRL MOST LIKELY ('57). Her final film credit was in SUMMER RUN ('74).

Commenting further to Mike Fitzgerald, Judy says, "When I was very small, I bought a palomino, Taffy, at an auction. He was the color of taffy and much blonder than Trigger. I've been riding all my life." Her ability as a rider allowed Judy to do some stunt double work in CATTLE ANNIE AND LITTLE BRITCHES and PONY EXPRESS RIDER. She appeared in numerous television guest roles, among them appearances on "Annie Oakley," "Make Room For Daddy," "Sugarfoot," "The Lone Ranger," "Lassie," "Adventures of Superman," "Rawhide," and "The Tall Men."

Nugent's favorite film role was in MAGNIFICENT OBSESSION, and her favorite television appearance was on "Rawhide." Her favorite performer was Rock Hudson.

Judy and actor Buck Taylor were married in 1961. The marriage lasted for some twenty years before breaking up. It produced four children: a daughter Tiffany, and sons, Adam, Matthew and Cooper. Daughter Tiffany has two children.

The three sons, of whom Judy says, "All my sons did ads for Wrangler Jeans. That's because all three have great butts—they got that from Buck. He was a great butt." Son Adam was married to June Lockhart's daughter Anne before his untimely death in a motorcycle accident. From this marriage there are two more grandchildren. Matthew is a Hollywood stuntman and double, and youngest son Cooper helps Judy run the Montana ranch.

Counted among those Judy admires, and her friends in the entertainment business, past and present, are Dub Taylor, her ex-father-in-law, of whom she called "my most favorite man in the whole world," Ken Curtis, "nobody ever said a bad word about Ken," actress Sherry Jackson, June Lockhart, daughter-in-law Anne Lockhart Nugent, and stuntman Mike Moroff.

Of life today, Judy says, "I love ranch life, the outdoors, and horses."

A true American cowgirl.

HELEN PARRISH

Helen Parrish got an early start in her film career by appearing in B-westerns. Legend has it that when Helen was either three or five years of age (depending on which of her reported birth dates one chooses to accept), she accompanied her mother and sister to a casting interview. The purpose of the trip was for her sister to apply for a role as the daughter of baseball great, Babe Ruth, in the 1927 film starring Babe, BABE COMES HOME. As luck would have it, the casting director selected Helen over her sister for the role. *(This event probably did little to promote sibling harmony.)*

Helen was born on March 12, 1923, in Columbus, Georgia. No information could be located as to Helen's father. Other members of her family were involved in the ownership of radio station WCLS in Columbus for many years. Her mother was actress Laura Parrish who passed away on August 15, 1977, at age ninety.

Helen's siblings all had Hollywood roots. Her two brothers, Robert and Gordon, and her sister Beverly were actors. Her mother, Laura Parrish, played minor roles from the 1920s and was a charter member of the Screen Actor's Guild. Brother Robert was the more renown of the family, who not only had an acting career, but also was a successful film editor who won two Oscars for his work in BATTLE OF MIDWAY, a documentary, and John Garfield's BODY AND SOUL

('47). He was nominated for a third Oscar for his work with ALL THE KING'S MEN ('49). He also worked as both a director and producer, and was the author of *Growing Up in Hollywood* and *Hollywood Doesn't Live Here Anymore*.

Following Helen's role as Babe Ruth's daughter, sources claim Helen was in some "Our Gang" comedies. This could not be verified, but Helen's sister Beverly, who lost out in the role of Babe Ruth's daughter, is credited with an "Our Gang" role.

Parrish's movie career as a child actress in western films, or with western actors, was pretty much limited to three films. She had roles with William Boyd in HIS FIRST COMMAND ('29), with John Wayne in THE BIG TRAIL ('30), and with Richard Dix in CIMARRON ('31). There followed a myriad of roles in some Deanna Durbin and Little Tough Guys films, and a variety of movies, none of which caused more than a ripple. Among them were BRIDE OF FRANKEN-STEIN ('35), CINDERELLA SWINGS IT ('43), and SIX LESSONS FROM MADAME LAZONGA ('41).

As an adult, Parrish moved on to leading roles in western features that included IN OLD CALI-FORNIA ('42) with John Wayne, and SUNSET SERENADE with Roy Rogers ('42). In 1948 she joined Charles Starrett and Smiley Burnette in QUICK ON THE TRIGGER. Helen's final film was THE WOLF HUNTERS ('49) with Kirby Grant. In 1942 Helen had a lead role in the Universal western serial, OVERLAND MAIL with Lon Chaney, Jr., Noah Beery, Jr., Noah Beery, Sr., and Don Terry.

Following the end of her film career, Helen played an active role in the newly-arrived television industry. She made many guest appearances, playing an active role in several shows. She was hostess of a popular program in New York, "The Hour Glass," for two years. In California, she hosted "This is Your Music" and served as women's editor to a popular early morning show, "Panorama Pacific." I don't know what, if anything, she knew about football, but one source credits her as doing a professional football telecast with football great Tom Harmon.

The year 1942 marked a significant event in Parrish's life as she married film writer Charles Lang. This marriage must have had some compatible moments as it lasted until 1954 and produced two children, a son and a daughter. In 1954 things "hit the fan." During a party in the couple's home, Lang allegedly discovered Helen and a man named Muzzy Marcellino in a compromising situation in the kitchen. In the contested divorce that ensued, Helen claimed she was verbally and physically abused by Lang following his discovery of her indiscretion. Lang countered with the claim that Parrish was possessed of overactive hormones and had been engaged in an adulterous relationship over a four-year period. The judge made no specific finding of adultery but did award custody of the two children to Lang, granting Parrish limited visitation rights.

In 1956 Helen decided to take another stab at married life. She was wed to television producer John Guedel, who produced the "Art Linkletter" and "Groucho Marx" programs.

In 1958 Parrish developed cancer, and on February 22, 1959, at the young age of 35, she passed away at Hollywood Presbyterian Hospital. Her *Variety* obituary notes Helen was survived by her husband and her two children from her marriage to Charles Lang.

GIGI PERREAU

"I qualify," remarked Gigi, at a recent Asheville Film Festival, as we discussed those juvenile entertainers who were to be included among the "Kid Kowboys." She does indeed. At age eight she was part of the cast of NEVER A DULL MOMENT ('50) along with Fred MacMurray, Irene Dunne, Andy Devine, and Natalie Wood, and as a teenager she teamed up with Will Rogers, Jr. in WILD HERITAGE ('58).

In late 1940, the Perreau family—consisting of Gigi's father, mother, and two year old brother—fled from German-occupied France where they had been living and arrived in Los Angeles. Shortly thereafter, on February 6, 1941, Ghislaine Elizabeth Marie Therese Perreau-Saussine entered the world.

After learning director Mervyn LeRoy was searching for a young girl who looked as if she might be of French extraction for a role in MADAME CURIE ('43), Gigi's mother took her young daughter to MGM where Gigi was immediately cast in the role of young Curie. Included among Perreau's approximately 40 films were GOD IS MY CO-PILOT ('45), GREEN DOLPHIN STREET ('47), BONZO GOES TO COLLEGE ('52), MAN IN THE GRAY FLANNEL SUIT ('56), and TAMMY TELL ME TRUE ('61). She also had roles in two television series, "The Betty Hutton Show" and "Follow the Sun." Counted among her stage roles were parts in "Barefoot in the Park" and "As You Like It." Among Gigi's numerous guest appearances on television included spots on "Perry Mason," "Alfred Hitchcock Presents," "Stagecoach West," "Laramie," "The Rebel," "Rawhide," "Gunsmoke," "My Three Sons," "Gomer Pyle, U.S.M.C.," "The Rifleman" and "The Brady Bunch." Her final film credit was in HIGH SEAS HIJACK ('78).

Gigi was first married at age 19 to Frank Gallo, heir of the famous California vineyards. This union produced two children, daughter Gina, and son Tony. She was later married to Gene deRuelle, formerly an assistant director on the "Kung Fu" television series. This marriage resulted in two more children, daughter Danielle and son Keith.

Gigi is a graduate of Immaculate Heart High School in Hollywood where she now devotes some of her time to teaching drama. She is active in community affairs and has received numerous honors and recognition for her work. She served as co-vice president of the Drama Teachers Association of Southern California; is a member of the board of directors for Theatricum Botanicum; is the recipient of the Milky Way Gold Star Award, the Film Daily Critics Award, and the Distinguished Alumnae Award of Immaculate Heart College; and is among those who have a star on the Hollywood Walk of Fame.

Gigi is a budding writer as she is working on her autobiography, *Everybody's Little Girl*. She resides in the Los Angeles area.

MICKEY RENTSCHLER

Mickey Rentschler is credited with 21 film roles during an eleven-year career as a juvenile player, with three of his films being B-westerns. Mickey's movie life commenced at age ten with a spot in

HIS PRIVATE SECRETARY ('33), a John Wayne non-western, and came to an end with an appearance in TWO GIRLS AND A SAILOR ('44) starring Gloria DeHaven, June Allyson, and Van Johnson.

Mickey was born Milton Edward Rentschler on October 6, 1923 in Detroit, Michigan, the son of Otto J. Rentschler and Marieta M. Ryan Rentschler. Both parents were also born in Michigan.

Rentschler's B-western roles included an excellent part in Bob Steele's BRAND OF HATE ('34), roles with Johnny Mack Brown in BRANDED A COWARD ('35) and with the "Three Mesquiteers" trio of Bob Steele, Tom Tyler, and Rufe Davis in WEST OF CIMARRON ('41). Among other films of note in which Mickey made appearances were KID MILLIONS ('34) with Eddie Cantor, THE SCARLET LETTER ('34) with Colleen Moore, THE ADVENTURES OF TOM SAWYER ('38) with Tommy Kelly, BOYS TOWN ('38) starring Spencer Tracy and Mickey Rooney, PECK'S BAD BOY AT THE CIRCUS ('38) with Tommy Kelly again, THE ADVENTURES OF HUCKLE-BERRY FINN ('39) a Mickey Rooney film, YOUNG TOM EDISON ('40) again with Rooney, and SEE HERE, PRIVATE HARGROVE ('44) with Robert Walker and Donna Reed.

Mickey passed away at age 45 on June 27, 1969. His home address at that time was 1451 West Holt Avenue in Pomona, California. The certificate of death states at the time of his death he was divorced. He died at the Veterans Administration Hospital in Long Beach, California after a confinement of approximately three months. The listed causes for Rentschler's death were hepatic coma, gastrointestinal bleeding, and cirrhosis of the liver.

Mickey's employment for the last four and one-half years of his life was as a distribution clerk for the U. S. Post Office. Information on Mickey's life from the time he left films in 1944 and his approximate date of working with the postal service remain a mystery. It is safe to assume that some time during that period was spent in the military since he was eligible for treatment at a Veterans Hospital and due to the fact he is buried at the Veterans Administration Cemetery in West Los Angeles, California.

DON KAY REYNOLDS

Don Kay Reynolds was one of three "Kid Kowboys" who appeared as "Little Beaver" in the "Red Ryder" western series. He first appeared in THE YELLOW ROSE OF TEXAS ('44) with Roy Rogers. This was followed by credits in ROMANCE OF THE WEST ('46) with Eddie Dean, SONG OF ARIZONA ('46) again with Roy Rogers, and a cast that included "Kid Kowboys" Tommy Cook, Tommy Ivo, and Michael Chapin. Other western films that followed were THE LAST ROUNDUP ('47) with Gene Autry, WHIRLWIND RAIDERS ('48) with Charles Starrett, ROLL, THUNDER, ROLL! and RIDE, RYDER, RIDE! ('49), THE COWBOY AND THE PRIZE-FIGHTER and THE FIGHTING REDHEAD ('50) all with Jim Bannon as part of the "Red Ryder" series, THE RED PONY ('49) with Robert Mitchum and Myrna Loy, STREETS OF GHOST TOWN ('50) with Charles Starrett, BEYOND THE PURPLE HILLS ('50) with Gene Autry, SNAKE RIVER DESPERADOS ('51) with Charles Starrett again, and THE PAINTED HILLS ('51) with Gary Gray and "Lassie."

Reynolds, who was known by the nickname "Little Brown Jug" throughout his career, was not an easy subject on which to obtain biographical information. Reportedly, he is still alive. Luther Hathcock, the "super sleuth" of obtaining information on western players of the past, reports that in the early '80s Reynolds was living in Ojai, California, where his wife Cindi was a town clerk in the water department at City Hall, and that later, "Jug" was working as a wrangler at Universal Studios. Within the past year, Hathcock wrote to Reynolds at what he felt was a correct current address. The letter was never returned by the post office, nor responded to by Reynolds. Several weeks later, the author tried the same tactics. Again, the letter was not returned by the postal authorities, nor answered by Reynolds.

Donn J. Moyer, the author of *Cowboy Cliffhangers* and the owner of Wild West Publishing Co. in Tacoma, Washington, who is an acquaintance of Don Kay's father, reports that sometime in the mid-90s he met "Jug" at the Western Washington Fair in Puyallup, Washington, where Don was working with "Have Trunk Will Travel," an elephant ride concession. Moyer also reported that Reynolds had previously opened a bar and restaurant in southern California, but that it was no longer open.

By far, the most revealing information on the life of "Little Brown Jug" was obtained during an interview conducted by Tom Nichols of radio station KVRE-FM of Hot Springs Village, Arkansas, in 1989. The interview occurred while Reynolds was a guest at the Memphis Film Festival. During the interview, Don Kay revealed: His father, Fess Reynolds, was born in Bowie, Texas, and was a famous rodeo performer who appeared in all the major events throughout the country. Fez specialized in bulldogging, roping, bareback riding, calf roping, and worked as a rodeo clown. The only event his father didn't compete in was bronc busting. Donn Moyer says Fess was a horse trainer.

Fess Reynolds moved to Vernon, Texas, where Don was born in 1937. Don says he was a rodeo performer at age two-and-a-half as a trick rider. He worked at his skills until he was 15 years old and was able to stand mounted on a Roman team (two horses) and jump over a car. In 1943 he accompanied his father to a rodeo at Madison Square Garden where the two of them were to perform. However, Don was not allowed to perform due to child labor laws as he was only five years old. While at Madison Square Garden, they met Roy Rogers who was the featured attraction. Roy observed Don practicing, and was impressed to the point that he invited Don and his father to come to Hollywood and assured them that Don would become the next "Little Beaver" due of Roy's influence at the studio.

Don and his father moved to Hollywood in 1944 and lived with Glenn Randall, the noted horse trainer, and his wife. He says Randall's wife became sort of a surrogate mother and enrolled him in school, as his father was indisposed due to a leg injury. (There is no reference to Don's mother during his lengthy interview).

The promise by Roy Rogers to see that Don Kay became the next "Little Beaver" fell through as Don says, "Republic thought I was too small." It wasn't long before another production company decided to do a new "Red Ryder" series, and Don was selected to join Jim Bannon in a series of 12 pictures. Only four were made as a contract dispute developed when the owner of the "Red Ryder" copyright insisted on a 25% cut of Reynolds' and Bannon's income. Don says his father vetoed the demand, and the series ended prematurely. Of his finally becoming "Little Beaver," Don remarked, "…I did it with no help from Roy Rogers."

Reynolds claims he left films at age 15 and returned to Vernon, Texas, to attend and graduate from Vernon High School. He joined the rodeo circuit, but quit when he was 18 years old. He later says it was in Belgium, when he was 21, that a horse stepped on him during a performance and due to the injury he quit the rodeo business, again.

Reynolds had a variety of jobs, other than those mentioned earlier, according to his interview with Tom Nichols. He says he worked on a ranch in Tehachapi, California, and became a blacksmith. He later moved to Ojai, California, where he says in addition to blacksmithing, he taught the art of horsemanship at a private boys' high school for many years. He also claims to have worked at the Disney Studios training camels and other animals that were used in films.

As to how he acquired the nickname "Little Brown Jug," Reynolds says that two of his cousins, sons of his father's brothers, were nicknamed "Whitey" and "Blackie," and that he became "Brownie." The brown jug part was added, he said, due to the Glenn Miller hit, "Little Brown Jug."

Of the cowboy stars he supported, Don had kind words for Bill Elliott and Jim Bannon. Asked about others, he said, "I wasn't too proud of Gene Autry." As a youngster, "Jug" said his heroes were Tim McCoy and Bill Elliott, but as he got older he most admired John Wayne and Gary Cooper.

During the interview, Don made reference to being a married man as he said he sometimes returns to Texas to visit his in-laws. After 31 years of marriage, Reynolds was divorced. He is the father of two sons and has two grandchildren. Don now resides in Texas.

JIMMY ROGERS

James Blake Rogers was born in New York City on July 25, 1915, the son of William Penn Rogers, better known as the famous Oklahoma humorist and motion picture star Will Rogers, and Betty Blake of Arkansas. Jimmy was the youngest of the Rogers' four children that included two other sons, Fred and Will, Jr., and a daughter Mary. Jimmy Rogers can be counted as a "Kid Kowboy" by virtue of a small part in a single film, when at age six he supported his famous father in DOUBLING FOR ROMEO ('21). Jimmy had made his screen debut a year earlier in a film titled THE STRANGE BOARDER ('20). Following his role in DOUBLING FOR ROMEO, there is a hiatus of twenty-one years before Jimmy is credited with another film role.

As an adult, Rogers joined his friend Noah Beery Jr. in a series of three light-hearted westerns: DUDES ARE PRETTY PEOPLE ('42), CALABOOSE ('42), and PRAIRIE CHICKENS ('43). Rogers then had support roles to William Boyd in the following six westerns: FALSE COLORS ('43), FORTY THIEVES ('44), TEXAS MASQUERADE ('44), RIDERS OF THE DEADLINE ('44), MYSTERY MAN ('44), and LUMBERJACK ('44).

Jimmy grew up in Pacific Palisades until the family moved to Santa Monica in 1929. He is credited with 14 years of formal education. His greatest passion was horses. He was a talented rider early on, and at age two he appeared on horseback at a benefit performance at New York's polo grounds. Later in life he was a member of one of Hollywood's polo teams.

Rogers served in the military during World War II. Following his Hollywood days, he was, for many years, a rancher in Kern County, California. After ending his ranching career, he trained show horses.

During an interview at the Memphis Film Festival during the 1980s, Jimmy offered the following notes of interest: despite his father's reputation as an astute businessman, it was his mother who made the financial decisions for the family; growing up, one of his closest friends was Maxine Jones, daughter of western star Buck Jones; and William Boyd and Andy Clyde were both very helpful in aiding him in his later acting roles. He said in his retirement years he was working on a book on the history of the Cherokee nation.

Jimmy was twice married. In 1936 he married Astrea Kemmler. This union produced three children, two sons and a daughter. The marriage ended with Astrea's death in 1987. In 1995 Jimmy wed for a second time, this time to Katharine Judith Braun. This marriage endured until Jimmy's death at his home in Bakersfield, California, on April 28, 2000. The causes of his death were cardiopulmonary arrest of 15 minutes duration, and non-Hodgkin's lymphoma, which he suffered from the final six months of his life. Jimmy was cremated, and his remains now lie at rest at the Will Rogers Memorial in Claremore, Oklahoma.

WILL ROGERS, JR.

Will Rogers, Jr. never gained the stature of his famous father, but he did play the role of a "Kid Kowboy" in two early B-westerns. In 1921 he supported Guinn "Big Boy" Williams in THE JACK RIDER and THE VENGEANCE TRAIL. His later Hollywood career was limited to appearances in only five films. He joined June Haver and Ray Bolger in LOOK FOR THE SILVER LINING ('49); played the role of his father in THE STORY OF WILL ROGERS ('52) with Jane Wyman; made an appearance in THE EDDIE CANTOR STORY ('53); again played the role of his father in THE BOY FROM OKLAHOMA ('54); and had a lead role in WILD HERITAGE ('58). He served as host of the television show "Good Morning" ('57) and appeared in "The Pioneers" ('63), the syndicated title of the first 194 episodes of "Death Valley Days."

Rogers was born in New York City on October 20, 1911, while his famous father was the headliner in the Ziegfeld Follies. The family later returned to California, and Will, Jr. graduated from Beverly Hills High School in 1931. He then attended Stanford University where he edited an off-campus newspaper, captained the polo team, was a member of the university debate team, and set a school record in the backstroke on the swimming team. He graduated in 1935 with a bachelor of arts degree. Shortly after Rogers' college graduation, his father died in an Alaskan plane crash. Will used part of his inheritance to become the editor/publisher of the *Beverly Hills Citizen*, and working with his brother Jimmy, the *Citizen* became one of the largest weekly newspapers in the west over the next 18 years.

In 1941 Will was appointed to the California Maritime Commission, and a year later he successfully ran as a Democrat and was elected to the U.S. Congress to represent southern California's 16th congressional district. While a member of Congress, he championed many liberal causes and was most active in his concern over the treatment of the Jews in Europe. In 1944 Will resigned from Congress to enter the U.S. Army. He became a platoon leader in a reconnaissance company of the 814th tank destroyer battalion of the seventh armored division. He rose to the rank of 1st lieutenant and was awarded a Bronze Star for heroism during the Battle of the Bulge. Later he was the recipient of a Purple Heart for injuries received during the Battle of the Ruhr.

From 1967-69, Will again served his government as special assistant to the commissioner of Indian affairs. Rogers' later years were spent on the lecture circuit and in serving as production consultant for the Tony Award-winning "Will Rogers Follies."

Will Rogers, Jr. married Collier Connell, whom he had met while a student at Stanford. The couple became advocates of the plight of the Navajos in Arizona, a concern possibly associated with Will's Cherokee heritage. Will and his wife adopted a 10-year-old Navajo boy, whom they renamed Clem, in honor of Will's grandfather. They later had a son, Carl. The Rogers' family donated the land for Will Rogers State Park in Pacific Palisades, California, and Will Rogers State Beach in Santa Monica.

MICKEY ROONEY

Mickey Rooney is not often associated with being one of the "Kid Kowboys," but he was indeed. Born Joe Yule, Jr. on September 23, 1920, in Brooklyn, New York, he was the only child of parents who were a vaudeville team. Mickey was on stage as part of the family act before his second birthday. Talented as a singer and dancer and adept at playing the piano and drums at an early age, he arrived in Hollywood in the late '20s to reportedly audition for a role in the "Our Gang" comedy series but was unsuccessful in his audition due to overacting. However, a film career did manifest itself and from 1927 to 1934, he appeared in over seventy comedy short subjects billed as Mickey McGuire. He made the first of his over 200 films in a short subject, NOT TO BE TRUSTED ('26) and is still active in the world of entertainment

Mickey's schooling was largely at Mrs. Lawlor's School for Professional Children. It was there he met Judy Garland, with whom he would co-star in several future films. His juvenile role in a western occurred in the Tom Mix oater MY PAL THE KING ('32), where he played a boy monarch rescued by Mix from the palace bad guys. Rooney also appeared with Buck Jones in HIGH SPEED ('32), a non-western.

He legally changed his name to Mickey Rooney in 1932, and he is probably best known to the movie public for his starring roles in the Andy Hardy series of some 15 films. Among the more notable of his numerous roles were his credits in A MIDSUMMER NIGHT'S DREAM ('35), BOYS TOWN ('38), THE ADVENTURES OF HUCKLEBERRY FINN ('39), BABES IN ARMS ('39), YOUNG TOM EDISON ('40), STRIKE UP THE BAND ('40), BABES ON BROADWAY ('41), A YANK AT ETON ('42), THE HUMAN COMEDY ('43), NATIONAL VELVET ('44), THE BRIDGE AT TOKO-RI ('54), REQUIEM FOR A HEAVYWEIGHT ('62), and THE BLACK

STALLION ('79). Rooney's work in films led to nominations for Academy Awards in BABES IN ARMS, THE HUMAN COMEDY, THE BOLD AND THE BRAVE, and THE BLACK STALLION. The Academy awarded him an honorary Oscar in 1938 and again in 1983.

Rooney's talents in the entertainment world were not limited to his acting career in Hollywood. He also worked as the producer of THE TWINKLE IN GOD'S EYE ('55), among other films. His work as a director included THE PRIVATE LIVES OF ADAM AND EVE ('61). He served as a writer with THE GODMOTHERS ('73) and THE OUTLAWS: LEGEND OF O. B. TAGGART ('94). He was the composer of SOUND OFF ('52). Among his numerous television guest appearances were stints on "The Tonight Show," "Wagon Train," "Andy Williams Show," "Rawhide," "The Fugitive," "The Carol Burnett Show," "The Love Boat," "The Golden Girls," "Murder, She Wrote," "The Simpsons," "ER," and "Larry King Live." He starred in two television sitcoms "Hey Milligan/The Mickey Rooney Show" ('54) and "Mickey" ('64) and later co-starred in the series "The Adventures of the Black Stallion."

Sources indicate Mickey was drafted into the armed forces during World War II. There is a hiatus in his film credits during 1945-46. Hence, if Uncle Sam did call, it is unlikely anyone was shooting at Mickey, as by that time the war was approaching an end.

Mickey has written two autobiographies, *i.e.* and *Life Is Too Short*. He won an Emmy for his role in the 1981 telefilm "Bill." He has performed in nightclubs and theatres. He co-starred with Ann Miller in the burlesque revue "Sugar Babies" nationwide and for a lengthy run on Broadway. In 1939 he was Hollywood's top box-office draw, unseating former titleholder Shirley Temple. Needless to say, this is an impressive resume for a kid from Brooklyn.

Mickey's personal life was a different story. Among his eight wives was a trip down the aisle with Carolyn Mitchell early in his career. Following Carolyn, he next wedded Ava Gardner, a union that lasted for sixteen months. Mickey's third spouse was Betty Jane Rase, a four-year sojourn. Wife number four was actress Martha Vickers, whose marriage to Rooney lasted for three years. Fifth in line to visit a justice of the peace with Mickey was Elaine Mahnken; they tolerated each other for six years.

Next to take the vows with Rooney was a woman named Barbara Ann Thompson. This relationship had an odd twist. The marriage lasted for eight years and produced four children. Barbara Ann then met her demise when she was done in by a murder-suicide perpetrated by Milos Milocevic. *We don't know if Mickey and Barbara Ann were still sharing the same "beauty rest" at the time, but suspect something must have been going on between Milos and Barbara Ann to cause such drastic action.*

Mickey and Marge Lane then entered into what was more a "sleep-over" than a marriage as it only lasted 100 days. Carolyn Hockett and Mickey tried it for five years before saying, "adios." Finally, in 1978 Rooney and January Chamberlin tied the knot and that marriage, at last reports, was still ongoing.

All of these liaisons, reportedly, resulted in nine children, not all by the same partner, but according to one of Rooney's biographers, Mattias Thuresson, "The Mick" fathered five sons and four daughters. The sons, says the aforementioned biographer, are Tim, an actor; Teddy, also an actor;

Mickey, Jr., an actor and musician; and Kyle and Jimmy, with no stated means of support. The daughters, reportedly, are Kimmy, Kelly, Kerry, and Jonelle. No information was proffered as to their station in life.

Some notes of possible interest.

• In discussing his marriages, Mickey does refer to his eight wives. However, Mattias Thuresson list nine women among those spouses. Maybe, when there are that many, it's easy to lose count.

• Mickey's son Teddy appeared with him in "Andy Hardy Comes Home" ('58), in the role of Andy Hardy, Jr.

• Mickey's father was Scottish-born vaudeville performer Joe Yule who played "Jiggs" in a series of "Jiggs and Maggie" Monogram films.

• Rooney lists his hobbies as golf and "playing the ponies."

• Mickey was among the actors considered for the role of Archie Bunker on "All in the Family."

In a recent article in a national publication Rooney alludes to his respect for women. In his autobiography *Life Is Too Short*, he discusses in some detail his and Don "Red" Barry's sexual relations with actresses Betty Grable and Joan Crawford in the backseats of their limos in the presence of their chauffeurs. *(Author's Note: There may be those among us that have used the backseat for similar purposes, but it's hard to visualize one who respects women writing about it publicly and naming names.)*

Mickey Rooney, a man who surely made millions during his long and successful career, was last seen on late night television "hawking" burial insurance.

Talent he possessed; class, he lacked.

BETSY KING ROSS

Betsy King Ross was one juvenile player who had only a brief career as a "Kid Kowboy." It was her choice to have no further Hollywood connections thereafter.

Elizabeth Ross was born in Saint Paul, Minnesota, on March 14, 1922. Her parents were Captain Joseph King Ross and Islay Isobel McKenzie. Her father was born in New York and was a noted horse trainer, and her mother was from Canada. Both parents were circus performers. Shortly after Betsy's birth, the family moved to Alamo, Texas. There, during her early school years, Betsy became an accomplished horseback rider. By the time she was eight years old, she was a champion trick rider for the Lewis Brothers' Circus, receiving top billing as "The Texas Tomboy." Her talent came to the attention of Hollywood, and it wasn't long afterwards that she made her movie debut.

Betsy's juvenile western film credits consist of supporting roles with George O'Brien in SMOKE

LIGHTNING ('33), the serial FIGHTING WITH KIT CARSON ('33) with Johnny Mack Brown, and the serial THE PHANTOM EMPIRE ('35) with Gene Autry and Frankie Darro. A feature version of the serial THE PHANTOM EMPIRE was released in 1940. Following her work in THE PHANTOM EMPIRE, Betsy told her parents she had no desire to continue acting, and her folks honored her position. Thus, it was "adios" to Hollywood for Betsy Ross King.

Betsy finished high school and went on to Northwestern University from which she graduated with a Bachelor's degree. On March 3, 1948, Betsy married Davis R. Day, a civil engineer. Soon after their marriage, the couple left to work with the Corps of Engineers and were involved with the reconstruction of Greece and Morocco following World War II. In 1954 they moved to Colombia, South America, where Day worked at building roads for the Corps of Engineers. The following year, Betsy was pregnant and wanted their child to be born in the United States, so she moved to Orlando, Florida, where she gave birth to the couple's son, Russell "Rusty" Day. Following the birth of their son, Betsy and the boy returned to Colombia, where on January 13, 1956, tragedy struck—Betsy's husband was killed in an avalanche while working in the mountains.

After her husband's death, Betsy moved to the Santa Monica, California, area where the family had earlier purchased a home to raise her son and continue her education. She obtained a Master's degree from U.C.L.A. Betsy later became a talented writer and researcher fluent in four languages. For many years she worked at U.C.L.A. and was medical editor for the Child Amputee Prosthetic Project. Her son became a physical education teacher. Betsy remained a widow for the rest of her life.

At age 67, Betsy passed away on October 4, 1989, at the Northridge Hospital in Northridge, California. The cause of her death is stated as malignant lymphoma, from which she suffered for the final four years of her life. Betsy had resided at 9749 Reseda Boulevard, # 10, in Northridge prior to her death. Betsy King Ross is buried at Oakwood Memorial Park, 22601 Lassen Street, Chatsworth, California. (Statistical information relating to her death was reported by her son Russell.)

FRED SALE, JR.

Fred Sale, Jr. was born in Atlanta, Georgia, on August 22, 1928. His mother, Dorothy Hale, a housewife, was born in Georgia, His father, Frederick Link Sale, Sr., was born in Chester, South Carolina, on May 2, 1902, and attended the University of Georgia where he excelled as a baseball pitcher. He was signed by the Pittsburgh Pirates, where he, according to *The Official Encyclopedia of Baseball*, had a brief undistinguished career in 1924 with a record of 0-0 in one game.

Following his stint in baseball, the senior Sale went to work for the Coca-Cola Company in Atlanta. In the early 1930s, Coca-Cola transferred him to the Los Angeles area, where Fred, Jr. was soon to become an actor. Fred, an only child, relates that he was dressed in a cowboy outfit (a recent Christmas present) and was with his mother at an antique shop when they were approached by a man who asked if they were interested in a movie career for Fred. The man happened to be Alan James, the western director. After some debate and ascertaining that the offer was legitimate, Fred soonafter was on screen with Ken Maynard in WHEELS OF DESTINY ('34). He went on to relate he was in numerous films after that, and his favorite was a role in A MIDSUMMER NIGHT'S DREAM ('35) with James Cagney and Joe E. Brown.

Fred received his early education in the California public school system and also attended classes at the studio where he says Mickey Rooney was always a disruptive force. He goes on to say that in 1933 an earthquake demolished his public school to the point where they all ended up in the basement and had to finish the year in tents. He graduated from Pomona High School and later attended El Camino Junior College.

With the advent of the Korean War *(uh, "police action")* Fred became a member of the U.S. Army. He was stationed at Fort Ord and The Presidio in California teaching weaponry during 1950 when his term was nearing its end. In a patriot fever, Sale insisted he wanted to see action. His request was honored, and he soon found himself amid the hostilities. It turned out to be a bad choice; Fred was severely wounded by an exploding mortar shell. As he was being airlifted to Hawaii for treatment for his wounds, he says he was being served a glass of chocolate milk by a nurse when the plane was suddenly hit by a violent typhoon. Fred's only casualty from this encounter was that he found himself covered with chocolate milk. Following treatment for his wounds in Hawaii and California, he received a medical disability discharge.

Fred then relocated in the Portland, Oregon area where he, like his father, was employed by the Coca-Cola Company.

Fred has been three times married. The first two he had no desire to discuss, but he has been married for 37 years to the former Nancy Budgett. The wedding took place in 1964 in Downey, California. Nancy is a former Brigham Young University student. Of Fred's earlier marriages, children Debbie, Freddy, and Casey resulted.

Following are some of Fred's recollections from the past, his days in Hollywood, and his life today:

• He was a member of the track team in school.

• All four of Sale's great-grandfathers fought in the Civil War.

• During his time in combat, Fred carried a replica of the "Stars and Bars" for good luck. (It didn't work.)

• Once while on the set, young Sale was wearing a cowboy hat when Buck Jones came over and reshaped it to look like the one he was wearing.

• Another time on the set, he was eating some Hershey "kisses" when he was joined by Warner Baxter. Despite many calls by the film crew for Baxter to return to work, he refused to leave until the "kisses" had all been consumed.

• Once when Billy Barty, the midget performer, was doubling him in a fall scene, Fred's mother thought it was her son in a real fall and rushed forward to try to catch him.

• Sale's favorite actors with whom he worked were James Cagney and Joe E. Brown.

• Fred's closest friend from his Hollywood days is Anita Louise.

• His activities today are hunting, fishing, and traveling the country in his Woodwind Travel Trailer.

• Fred and Nancy now reside in Chehalis, Washington.

As we ended our conversation, Fred said, "This is the longest I have ever talked in my life."

ANDY SHUFORD

Andy Shuford may have been a hero to thousands of B-western fans as a "Kid Kowboy" in the early 1930s, but he became a hero to a whole nation later on in life.

Little is known of Andy's early life. He was born in Helena, Arkansas, on December 16, 1917, and probably arrived in Hollywood in the late 1920s. Some sources credit him with unbilled roles in six "Our Gang" comedies. His first foray into the world of western films was as a supporting member of the cast in John Wayne's first starring movie, THE BIG TRAIL ('30). During his brief time in Hollywood, Andy appeared in three non-westerns: the Wallace Beery/Jackie Cooper classic, THE CHAMP, THE EASIEST WAY with Robert Montgomery and Constance Bennett, and finished his film career in 1932's WHEN A FELLOW NEEDS A FRIEND, in which he played the role of a bully harassing Jackie Cooper.

Shuford's B-western roles included GOD'S COUNTRY AND THE MAN and A RIDER OF THE PLAINS ('31) with Tom Tyler, THE GREAT MEADOW ('31) with Johnny Mack Brown and HEADIN' FOR TROUBLE ('31) with Bob Custer. Andy's greatest impacts in the world of B-westerns were his roles in a series of eight oaters with Bill Cody during the years 1931-1933. These films established Shuford as one of the more popular "Kid Kowboys." The series consisted of DUGAN OF THE BAD LANDS, LAND OF WANTED MEN, THE MONTANA KID, OKLAHOMA JIM, THE GHOST CITY, LAW OF THE NORTH, MASON OF THE MOUNTED, and TEXAS PIONEERS.

Bill Cody, Jr., who succeeded Shuford as his father's young sidekick, related the following comments about Shuford during an interview with premier western film historian, Luther Hathcock: "Andy looked like the real American boy—slender, friendly, and happy. He was older than me, yet he treated me as a peer at a time when most boys are impressed with being older than the other kid." The young Cody went on to relate that Andy was good with his lines and a breeze for directors to work with. By 1934 Andy Shuford's days in Hollywood were finished.

It was Shuford's career after Hollywood that made him a true hero to his country. At age eighteen he enlisted in the U. S. Army Air Corp and became a career officer. Flying B-17s out of England during World War II, Shuford was credited with thirty-five missions. He earned the Distinguished Flying Cross (the air medal with five clusters), the Purple Heart, and a superior rating as a pilot (the nation's highest).

Shuford never returned to Hollywood. After his army career was over, he settled down to life in Tennessee. Colonel William "Andy" Shuford spent his final years in Monteagle, Tennessee, and in the veterans' hospital in Murfreesboro, Tennessee. He passed away on May 19, 1995, at Monteagle, Tennessee.

An enigma, this popular child actor and highly-decorated war hero rated no mention in *Variety's* obituary, and information about life before his Hollywood career and after his war service is not easily located. Hence, we don't know anything of Andy's parents, his youth, whether or not he had siblings, whether he married, or had children.

DEAN STOCKWELL

Dean Stockwell was born Robert Stockwell on March 5, 1936, in Hollywood, California. His parents were Harry Stockwell and Nina Olivette who were both actors. Harry Stockwell was also a singer and provided the speaking and singing voice for "Prince Charming" in the Disney classic, SNOW WHITE AND THE SEVEN DWARFS. The late actor Guy Stockwell is a brother to Dean.

Stockwell has had a long, if not exactly spectacular, career both in films and on television. His first screen appearance was in ANCHORS AWEIGH ('45) starring Gene Kelly and Frank Sinatra. Dean is credited with well over 100 films; many are the made-for-television variety.

Some of Dean's movie credits worthy of note: He appeared in the highly-awarded GENTLEMAN'S AGREEMENT ('47) with Gregory Peck. He played the role of "Nick Charles, Jr." with William Powell and Myrna Loy in SONG OF THE THIN MAN ('47). In 1948 he starred in one of his more memorable roles in THE BOY WITH GREEN HAIR. Regarding this film, one source states: "During the filming of THE BOY WITH GREEN HAIR, Dean, then twelve, had to wear two wigs during the filming of the movie: one loose, and one tight-fitting that would simulate a shaved head. When the final scene was shot and the film was being wrapped up, Dean asked for the tight-fitting wig. It was given to him, and he asked if he could do whatever he wanted with it. Told that he could, he snatched it off his head, threw it on the ground, and jumped all over it, yelling like a crazy Comanche. The skintight hairpiece had been sheer torture."

Dean had a substantial role in the Fred MacMurray western GUN FOR A COWARD ('56) and in the Katharine Hepburn/Jason Robards film LONG DAYS JOURNEY INTO NIGHT ('62). In 1986 he had a role in ECSTASY. He joined up with Eddie Murphy in BEVERLY HILLS COP II ('87). One of his film highlights occurred when he played a mob boss in MARRIED TO THE MOB ('88), for which he was nominated for an Oscar. In THE RAINMAKER ('97) he played a judge, and in BUFFALO SOLDIERS ('01) he portrayed a general. He last appeared in FACE TO FACE ('01), and there are probably more to come.

In addition to his film credits, none of which are earth shakers, his television guest appearances have been numerous. Among those are "The Restless Gun," "Wagon Train," "Bonanza," "McCloud," "Mission Impossible," "The A-Team," "Miami Vice," "The Twilight Zone," and "Murder, She

Wrote."

Stockwell's "Kid Kowboy" roles were few. He appeared in STARS IN MY CROWN ('50) with Joel McCrea, and he did have a good role as a spoiled kid in the McCrea oater, CATTLE DRIVE ('51). During this period he is reported to have traveled around the country working at odd jobs until he ended up in New York where he won high praise for his performance as a college boy killer in the Broadway production of "Compulsion." He later repeated his role in the film version, COMPULSION ('59), which won him an award at the Cannes Film Festival. He won a second Cannes Award in 1962 for his role in LONG DAY'S JOURNEY INTO NIGHT.

Then it was basically "adios" to films for a period when he was generally reported to be having personal problems. Other sources hinted that these problems were drug related. He later returned for a third Hollywood session, first playing minor roles, then achieving greater success with positive roles in DUNE ('84) with Jose Ferrer, PARIS TEXAS ('84) with Harry Dean Stanton, BLUE VELVET ('86) with Kyle MacLachlan, GARDEN OF STONE ('87) with James Caan, and an acclaimed cameo appearance in TUCKER: THE MAN AND HIS DREAM ('88) with Jeff Bridges. In 1982 Dean served as both writer and director and had an acting role in the film HUMAN HIGHWAY.

From 1960-1964 Stockwell was married to actress Millie Perkins, who gained some measure of fame for her role in THE DAIRY OF ANNE FRANK ('59). He later married a second wife, Joy, and reportedly fathered a son and a daughter.

JOE STRAUCH, JR.

Joe Strauch, Jr. was a "Kid Kowboy" closely associated in westerns with Gene Autry and Smiley Burnette. His western film credits consist of five oaters with Gene: UNDER FIESTA STARS ('41), HEART OF THE RIO GRANDE ('42), HOME IN WYOMIN' ('42), CALL OF THE CANYON ('42), and BELLS OF CAPISTRANO ('42). His only other western credit was BENEATH WESTERN SKIES ('44) with Bob Livingston and Smiley Burnette.

Joe's cast credits show he used almost as many names as he had films. He was billed as Joseph Strauch, Jr., Joseph C. "Tadpole" Strauch, Joseph Strauch, and Joe Strauch, Jr. However, in all of his western films, save one, he was known onscreen as "Tadpole," a junior version of Smiley "Frog" Burnette.

Strauch's non-western credits are limited to four roles. He made his debut in TWO TOO YOUNG ('36) and next appeared in FIGHTIN' FOOLS ('41), both "Our Gang" short subjects where he was billed as "Tubby." Reportedly, he also doubled "Spanky" McFarland in additional "Our Gangs." Other films consisted of a role in THIS TIME FOR KEEPS ('42) with Esther Williams and Jimmy Durante. He apparently finished out his Hollywood career in an un-billed spot as a "fat kid" in IF WINTER COMES ('47) with Walter Pidgeon and Deborah Kerr.

Born Joseph George Strauch, Jr. on May 18, 1929 (not 1930 as widely reported), in Chicago, Illinois, he was the son of German-Austrian parents, Joseph George Strauch and Ella Louise Schaefer

Strauch. Both parents were natives of the state of Illinois.

Joe was married to Mary Jane Strauch, and at the time of his death they resided at 1342 Poe Lane, San Jose, California. From 1953-1956 he served in the U.S. Military. During the final eight years of his life, Strauch was employed as a salesman for the J.C. Penney Company.

On May 23, 1986, Joe was in surgery for a coronary artery bypass graft. Eight days later, on May 31, 1986, he passed away at the Stanford Hospital in Stanford, California. The stated causes of his death were cardiac arrhythmia from which he suffered for twenty minutes, myocardiel failure for the eight days post surgery, and coronary artery disease, which had been present for ten years. On June 5, 1986, "Tadpole" was laid to rest at Holy Cross Cemetery in Culver City, California.

BEVERLY WASHBURN

Beverly Washburn proved to be a most gracious lady and a delight to speak with during our interview. She was born in Los Angeles, California, on November 25, 1943, and now lives in Henderson, Nevada (*close to all those nickel slot machines that love taking my money*).

Beverly's father, Howard Washburn, was a government employee and a Chicago native. Her mother, Marian, was from Wisconsin. Before Beverly was born the family was living in Chicago, but due to health problems with one of Beverly's older sisters they made the move to California.

There were five children in the Washburn family, with Beverly being the youngest. She had two brothers and two sisters, all now deceased. One sister acted under the screen name Audrey Allen, and a brother George was also an actor. George and Beverly were both part of the cast of the film PIT STOP ('69).

Beverly says she owes her entry into films to "Range Rider" Jock Mahoney. It seems Beverly was part of an amateur troupe giving a performance in Long Beach, California, when she met Jock, and obviously made an impression on him. Some time later, Beverly was part of a group waiting to audition for a role at the studio when Jock walked in. After being told why she was there, Jock walked into the office and convinced the casting director that Beverly was the person for the role. Beverly says Jock greatly enhanced her talents and abilities to insure she was hired.

Washburn's first credited role was in THE KILLER THAT STALKED NEW YORK ('50) with B-heroine Evelyn Keyes. Beverly's juvenile western credits include SHANE ('53) with Alan Ladd and Jean Arthur, THE LONE RANGER ('56) with Clayton Moore and Jay Silverheels, and OLD YELLER ('57) with Dorothy McGuire and Fess Parker.

Listed among her other film credits are roles in HERE COMES THE GROOM ('51) with Bing Crosby and Jane Wyman, SUPERMAN AND THE MOLE MEN ('51) with George Reeves and Phyllis Coates, THE GREATEST SHOW ON EARTH ('52) with a cast that included Jimmy Stewart. Charlton Heston, and Betty Hutton, and THE JUGGLER ('53) with Kirk Douglas.

Beverly was also part of the cast of a film, along with Lon Chaney Jr., which the producers apparently couldn't make up their minds on the title, but one I hope never to view. It appeared on marquees as either SPIDER BABY, THE MADDEST STORY EVER TOLD, ATTACK OF THE LIVER EATERS, CANNIBAL ORGY, or LIVER EATERS ('64) Her final credit was WHEN THE LINE GOES THROUGH ('73).

Washburn had roles on two television series, "Professional Father" ('55) and "The New Loretta Young Show" ('62). Television guest roles included "The Jack Benny Program," "Letter to Loretta," "Fury," "Zane Grey Theater," "Wagon Train," "The Texan," "Alcoa Presents," "Leave it to Beaver," "Star Trek," "The Streets of San Francisco," and "Scarecrow and Mrs. King."

Unlike many of the child actors, Beverly says she never attended a studio school. She elected to attend public schools and McEwer, a private high school. Her work, other than acting, has included being a secretary, a receptionist, and a massage therapist. Her hobbies and activities include movies, reading, tennis, crafts, and the outdoors.

Beverly has been twice married. Her first trip down the aisle was with a musician named Patrick. She is currently married to Michael, a sales manager. There are no children from either marriage, but she has cats and dogs, none of which ever want to use the family car or listen to loud rap "music."

During her movie career Beverly was awarded several honors. Being sponsored by Jack Benny, she won the 12th Annual Deb Star contest. She was the recipient of an award by the Hair-Make-Up Art Academy, and in 1952 she was voted one of the top five juvenile actors as part of the Box Office Blue Ribbon Award sponsored by the New York Film Dealers Association. Her favorite role, she says, was in OLD YELLER, and her favorite performers were Loretta Young and Gene Hackman.

Among her many friends in the entertainment industry with whom she keeps in touch are Tony Dow, Lauren Chapin, Sharon Baird, Tommy Kirk, and Cynthia Pepper.

Beverly is currently putting the finishing touches on a book, an autobiography on her time as a child star.

BOBS WATSON

Bobs Watson is his true name because his father wished to distinguish him from another actor named Bob Watson. He was born in Los Angeles on November 16, 1930, one of nine Watson children—five brothers and three sisters—who, as well as their parents, appeared in films, mainly in extra roles.

Watson began his film career with roles in a couple of "Our Gang" comedy shorts. Other films of note in which he appeared include SHOW BOAT ('36) with Irene Dunne, OUR GANG FOLLIES ('38), a reunion film with former players of the series, YOUNG DR. KILDARE ('38), CALLING DR. KILDARE ('39), and DR. KILDARE'S CRISIS ('40) with Lew Ayres, SCATTERGOOD PULLS THE STRINGS ('41)) with Guy Kibbee, and WHAT EVER HAPPENED TO BABY JANE

('62) with Bette Davis and Joan Crawford.

Watson made but two appearances in westerns. He had juvenile support roles in DODGE CITY ('39) with Errol Flynn, and in WYOMING ('40) with Wallace Beery. He was best known for his ability to cry on cue and was nicknamed "The Crybaby of Hollywood" following his role as "Pee Wee" in BOYS TOWN ('38) and MEN OF BOYS TOWN ('41). It was during the filming of BOYS TOWN that Bobs got to meet the famous Father Flanagan.

Bobs was part of the cast for the television series, "Hot Off the Wire," and had a number of guest appearances on television, including spots on "The Virginian," "Grindl," "The Beverly Hillbillies," "The F. B. I.," "Green Acres," "Please Don't Eat the Daisies," and "The Mother-in-Law."

When film roles began to dwindle, Bobs' father, J. C. Watson, became an itinerant street preacher, taking Bobs with him. This led to Bobs' later enrolling in the Claremont School of Theology and becoming an ordained minister. Later in life, he became the pastor at churches in Burbank and La Canada, California. He retired in June 1997, after 30 years as a Methodist minister.

Watson and his wife Jaye were the parents of three sons. In 1997 Bobs was diagnosed with prostate cancer, a disease that took his life on June 27, 1999, at Laguna Beach, California.

TWINKLE WATTS

In a film career that covered only three years, Twinkle Watts appeared in ten B-westerns. Her western films consisted of supporting roles in THE MAN FROM RIO GRANDE ('43), CANYON CITY ('43), CALIFORNIA JOE ('43), and OUTLAWS OF SANTA FE ('44), all with Don Barry as the lead. These were followed by SILVER CITY KID ('44), STAGECOACH TO MONTEREY ('44), SHERIFF OF SUNDOWN ('44), TOPEKA TERROR ('45), CORPUS CHRISTI BANDITS ('45), and TRAIL OF KIT CARSON ('45)—all with Allan Lane in the star role. *Hence, all of Twinkle's oaters were with either Barry or Lane, an exposure according to the many western players to whom I have spoken, tantamount to a violation of the 8th Amendment of the United States' Constitution banning cruel and unusual punishment.*

Watts managed three other film appearances in the short while she was in Hollywood. She had uncredited roles in LAKE PLACID SERENADE ('44) with Vera Vague and Vera Hruba Ralston, THE WOMAN WHO CAME BACK ('45) with Nancy Kelly and John Loder, and in a film with a most appropriate title, A GUY COULD CHANGE ('46) with Allan Lane in a non-western. Thus, Twinkle's movie career was at an end in spite of a 1944 studio press release stating she had been signed to a long-term contract.

There is ample evidence Twinkle was multi-talented, but she remains an enigma in that many of the facts garnered on her life seem to appear in conflict. In 1988 she was a guest at the Knoxville Western Film Festival and as part of a panel who answered questions posed by fans. During the guest star panel, Twinkle alluded to the fact that she was from New York. In response to how she got her start in Hollywood, she stated she had been performing professionally as an ice skater since the age of four years, and that in 1942, while performing as a star in New York City in "Stars on Ice," she was "discovered" by Herbert J. Yates, president of Republic Studio, who brought her to Hollywood and signed her to a contract. In her first film, THE MAN FROM RIO GRANDE, Republic managed to work scenes of Twinkle's ice skating talents into this B-western. Cast members seemed to enjoy Twinkle's talents on blades as the scenes were being played, but Don Barry, the film's star, had his considerable ego bruised when someone other than he was the center of attention. In his future references to Twinkle, he referred to her as "Winkle Twats."

At Knoxville, Twinkle volunteered that her true name was indeed Twinkle Watts, and that she had a sister whose name was Kilo Watts. (*A comment that would seem to indicate either her parents had weird senses of humor, or both were as crazy as a couple of pet crows.*) Twinkle stated further that Kilo became a concert violinist. (*However, there is no need to question the parents' sanity as the author has just learned from a highly reliable source that Twinkle Watts and Kilo Watts are not true names.*)

Twinkle introduced a man from the audience as her husband "John." Whether he was her only husband, or if Twinkle ever had children, remains a mystery, After her film career, Twinkle said she continued ice skating, and performed in stage productions and ballet. When asked if her mother was a pushy "stage mother," Twinkle replied in the affirmative.

Asked what she remembered of some of the actors and actresses she worked with, Twinkle remembered Wally Vernon's humor, Helen Talbot reading to her, and Peggy Stewart being nice to her. (*Peggy Stewart is nice to everyone*). Her favorite actors and actresses, she said, were John Wayne and Bette Davis.

From a studio press release in 1944, we are told that Twinkle was roller skating at age two, "although as an infant she was required to live in an oxygen tent to save her from a malady which physicians never diagnosed." Two years later another press release informs us that at age one Twinkle was stricken with polio and never expected to walk again.

Republic informs us in a 1943 press release that Twinkle achieved fame in Chicago as the national junior bowling champion before coming to Hollywood. Three years later, in 1946, Republic lets us know more of Twinkle's skills: "She learned to bowl purely by accident. Her father at one time ran a coffee shop in Hollywood and little Twinkle amused herself by rolling duck pins in the mornings with the pin boys." And, "At the age of five, Twinkle defeated the junior singles champion of America in a three game exhibition match held in Chicago, Illinois, after which her parents took her on a tour of the country."

There's more from Republic: "As a skater, she has starred at Madison Square Garden and has skated on exhibition tours throughout the country. But acting is only one of the accomplishments of the little blond star. She is a champion bowler, nationally known ice skater, ballet dancer and singer."

So, now we have a synopsis of Twinkle's life up to age five: She suffered from polio and it was feared she would never walk; she lived in an oxygen tent suffering from an undiagnosed malady; she was a roller skating whiz, a figure skating star, a national champion bowler, a singer of note, and a ballet star. She toured the country as both a bowler and a skater; grew up in New York, Chicago, or Hollywood, and became a "Kid Kowboy."

And I own this bridge in Brooklyn that I am wiling to sell.

BOBBY WINKLER

Robert "Bobby" Winkler was born in Chicago, Illinois, February 12, 1927, as Robert Winckler. He made his Hollywood debut at the age of four after being introduced to Hal Roach by the then-wife of comedian Charlie Chaplin, Mildred Harris Chaplin. As was the case for many of the juvenile players of those days, Bobby was a member of the "Our Gang" group, appearing in six of the popular comedy shorts.

As a youngster, Winkler's roles in westerns consisted of nine appearances in oaters: ARIZONA WILDCAT ('38) with Jane Withers and Leo Carrillo, BLUE MONTANA SKIES ('39) with Gene Autry, RIDERS OF PASCO BASIN ('40) with Johnny Mack Brown, GUN CODE ('40) with Tim McCoy, CHEROKEE STRIP ('40) with Richard Dix, THE WILDCAT OF TUCSON ('40) with Bill Elliott, THE LONE RIDER RIDES ON ('41) with George Houston, PALS OF THE PECOS ('41) with the Three Mesquiteer trio of Bob Steele, Bob Livingston and Rufe Davis, and BAD MEN OF MISSOURI ('41) with Dennis Morgan and Jane Wyman. Winkler made his final appearance in a western as a young adult with Johnny Mack Brown in PRAIRIE EXPRESS ('47). He is credited with a role in the serial DAREDEVILS OF THE RED CIRCLE ('39) with cast members that included such familiar names as Herman Brix, Dave Sharpe and Carole Landis.

Winkler's film roles were not limited to comedies, westerns and serials. He appeared in many high-quality films supporting some of Hollywood's legends as a cast member in BOYS TOWN ('38) with Spencer Tracy and Mickey Rooney, I AM A CRIMINAL ('38) with John Carroll and Mary Kornman, BABES IN ARMS ('39) with Mickey Rooney and Judy Garland, CITY FOR CONQUEST ('40) with James Cagney, Ann Sheridan and Bob Steele, KNUTE ROCKNE ALL AMERICAN ('40) with Pat O'Brien and Ronald Reagan, THE WAGONS ROLL AT NIGHT ('41) with Humphrey Bogart, LIFE BEGINS FOR ANDY HARDY ('41) with Mickey Rooney and Judy Garland, SULLIVAN'S TRAVELS ('42) with Joel McCrea and Veronica Lake, THIS GUN FOR HIRE ('42) with Alan Ladd and Veronica Lake, THE PRIDE OF THE YANKEES ('42) with Gary Cooper, and THE IRON MAJOR ('43) with Pat O'Brien. Bobby's final film was with Burt Lancaster and Yvonne DeCarlo in CRISS CROSS ('49) In addition to his film career, Winkler was active in both radio and television.

Bobby's early education was obtained at the Hollywood Professional School. After leaving the world of entertainment, Winkler attended law school and became a practicing attorney, representing many of the people he had worked with both in front of and behind the cameras. This endeavor must have provided unlimited opportunities and a lucrative income.

Bobby was married to Elizabeth Sturm, a union that produce two children, a daughter Patricia Winckler, and a son William Winckler, a Hollywood producer and director.

Bobby Winkler passed away on December 28, 1989, in Woodland Hills, California, from stomach cancer.

JANE WITHERS

She may have played "Avis" to Shirley Temple's "Hertz," but Jane Withers could also lay claim to being one of the "Kid Kowboys." As a juvenile actress she had western film credits in WILD AND WOOLLY ('37) with Walter Brennan, THE ARIZONA WILDCAT ('38) with Leo Carrillo, and SHOOTING HIGH ('40) with Gene Autry.

Jane was born in Atlanta, Georgia, on April 12, 1926, and had already performed in vaudeville and on radio when she made her film debut at age six in HANDLE WITH CARE ('32) with James Dunn. During 1933-34 she provided the voice for the cartoon character "Willie Whopper," but it was her role in BRIGHT EYES ('34) as the bratty rival to Shirley Temple that caused her Hollywood career to take off. During the next several decades she had roles in over fifty films, none of them of the blockbuster variety, but she must have been doing something right, because in 1938 she was one of the top-ten box office stars.

Jane's heyday in films lasted from the late 1930s to the mid-1940s when she was cast as a tomboy in CHICKEN WAGON FAMILY ('39), a junior miss in SMALL TOWN DEB ('41) and a young leading lady in AFFAIRS OF GERALDINE ('46). Her career as an adult actress was less than spectacular, although she had good roles in GIANT ('56) with Elizabeth Taylor, Rock Hudson, and James Dean, and CAPTAIN NEWMAN M.D. ('63) supporting Gregory Peck and Tony Curtis.

Withers' credited guest television appearances include stints on "The United States Steel Hour," "The Alfred Hitchcock Hour," "The Munsters," "The Love Boat," "Hart to Hart," and "Murder, She Wrote." Jane is probably best known for her role as "Josephine the Plumber" in the Comet cleanser television commercials for several years.

In 1947 Jane married for the first time. Her husband, William Moss, was a millionaire *(a good choice if one marries)*. Jane then retired to his hometown of Big Springs, Texas. Three children resulted from this union: a daughter Wendy, and two sons, William III and Randy. The couple divorced in 1954. The following year Jane became a bride for the second time when she and Kenneth Errair tied the knot. Errair was once a member of The Four Freshmen singing group and later became a lawyer. The couple became parents to a son, Kenneth, and a daughter, Kendall. In 1968 Errair, along with a number of others, was killed in a California plane crash. Jane later sued and was awarded a $200,000 settlement.

Jane has a hobby that she has kept her busy for 70 years—she collects Hollywood memorabilia, including props, costumes, and entire sets from the films in which she appeared. Jane resides in Hollywood and is actively involved in community affairs. She has served on the boards of the American Cancer Society and the Hollywood Chamber of Commerce, and she is a trustee of Hollywood's Church of Religious Science. David Ragan, in his *Who's Who in Hollywood*, comments that Jane has never smoked, nor drank, and is religious to the point of saying grace before every meal, even before a business luncheon at the Brown Derby.

ET AL

There are numerous others among the juvenile actors who enjoyed supporting roles in western films. Some are credited with but a single appearance, while others had a more extensive career in the world of entertainment. Unfortunately, for whatever reasons, many of those players, after their brief moments of fame, disappeared from public view, leaving fans with little information about their lives beyond the camera. After exhaustive research by the author and consultations with many of those considered the more knowledgeable of western film historians, there is still much lacking to report on the life and times of these "Kid Kowboys."

As Janet Lorenz, director of the National Film Information Service of the Margaret Herrick Library, Academy of Motion Picture Arts and Sciences, the premier source of motion picture information, wrote: "I'm afraid I don't have very good news to report. I have checked every file and reference source I can think of and I haven't been able to turn up even a scrap of information on any of the names on your list." So, for what little we know, here are notes on those who have vanished, or have proven to be unavailable.

SYLVIA ARSLAN

Of the seven film appearances credited to juvenile player Sylvia Arslan, two are of the "Kid Kowboy" variety. She made her film debut in MOON OVER HER SHOULDER ('41), with Dan Dailey and Lynn Bari. Over the next five years she continued with roles in four non-western movies in which she supported some of Hollywood's leading players. Included in this list are appearances in MR. SKEFFINGTON ('44) with Bette Davis and Claude Rains, IN OUR TIME ('44) with Ida Lupino and Paul Henreid, and HUMORESQUE ('46), her final credit, with John Garfield and Joan Crawford. Her western films are THE GREAT STAGECOACH ROBBERY ('45) with Bill Elliott and Bobby Blake, and SHERIFF OF CIMARRON ('45) with Sunset Carson and Linda Stirling. Obtaining information on the personal life of Sylvia Arslan was an impossible task.

BOBBY BEERS

Robert "Bobby" Beers played in the Roy Rogers' oater, SOUTH OF SANTA FE ('42). He is also credited with a role in LADY IN THE DARK ('44) with Ray Milland and Ginger Rogers. The only information located on Beers was a date of birth of July 17, 1928, and a death date of March 27, 1986, in San Francisco, California.

COPE BORDEN

Cope Borden appeared in a single western support role as a juvenile actor in TEXAS JACK ('35), a Jack Perrin oater. Additional information on this "Kid Kowboy" was not to be found.

BILLY BURRUD

William James Burrud was born January 12, 1925, in Hollywood, California. He had a brief fling as a "Kid Kowboy" in a support role to Buck Jones in THE COWBOY AND THE KID ('36), and to Richard Dix in IT HAPPENED IN HOLLYWOOD ('37). Among other films of note in which Burrud had roles are MAGNIFICENT BRUTE ('36) with Victor McLaglin, PRIDE OF THE MARINES ('36) with John Garfield and Eleanor Parker, CAPTAIN COURAGEOUS ('37) with Spencer Tracy, THE NIGHT HAWK ('38) with Bob Livingston, and a final un-credited role in HITLER'S CHILDREN ('42) with Tim Holt and Bonita Granville.

Following a hiatus of 16 years, during which time no information was found regarding the life of Billy Burrud, he is credited with serving as either host, producer, or moderator of several television series, including "Treasure" ('58), "Thrill Hunters" ('66), "Animal World" ('68), "Safari to Adventure" ('69), "The Challenging Sea" ('69), "The Great Apes" ('70), "World of the Sea" ('70), and "The World of Reptiles" ('71).

Billy is the father of actor-director, John Burrud. It could have been Burrud's fascination with the sea that contributed to his demise. On July 12, 1990, while swimming in the Pacific Ocean at Sunset Beach, California, he suffered a fatal heart attack.

BILLY BUTTS

Born September 8, 1919, in Dallas, Texas, Billy Charles Allen Butts was one of the "Kid Kowboys" who played largely in the silent film era. Little information is available on Butts, howver his father's name was Charles A. Butts, an indication Butts was Billy's true surname. Billy's mother was Madelle Garnder. Reportedly, he returned to Texas and attended Wonderland Park High School. Later, it is said he took some stage training, but no evidence could be found that his career in the world of entertainment continued after his Hollywood days. As was the case with many of the juvenile players of those early days, Billy is credited with two "Our Gang" appearances.

Billy made the first of his three western support roles with cowboy star Fred Thomson. His initial film was THE TOUGH GUY ('26), followed by THE TWO-GUN MAN and LONE HAND SAUNDERS, both also in 1926. Next in order are LAND BEYOND THE LAW ('27) with Ken Maynard, THE LAST OUTLAW ('27) with Gary Cooper, WILD WEST ROMANCE ('28) with Rex Bell, THE BLACK ACE ('28) with Don Coleman, TAKING A CHANCE ('28) with Rex Bell again, LONE STAR RANGER ('30) with George O'Brien, and SCARLET RIVER ('33) with Tom Keene.

During his relatively short Hollywood stay, Billy did have appearances in some non-westerns, among them are UNCLE TOM'S CABIN ('26) with Virginia Grey, NONE BUT THE BRAVE ('28), ALIAS JIMMY VALENTINE ('28) with William Haines, and ARE THESE OUR CHILDREN? ('31) with Rochelle Hudson.

What happened to Billy Butts following his "Kid Kowboy" days remains an enigma.

RALPH HOOPES

In a Hollywood career that appears to have lasted for only six years, and four film credits, Ralph Hoopes had two appearances in "Kid Kowboy" roles. He supported Bob Steele in RIDERS OF THE SAGE ('39), and Jack Randall in WILD HORSE RANGE ('40). Ralph's other Hollywood credits are roles with Jimmy Lydon in HENRY ALDRICH, BOY SCOUT ('44), and with Preston Foster in TWICE BLESSED ('45). After a 20-year hiatus, he is credited with a television guest role on "Baretta," and a role in the television film ROSETTI AND RYAN: MEN WHO LOVED WOMEN ('77).

Little information on Ralph Goss Hoopes could be found. He was born in Missouri on October 19, 1926, and died on January 16, 1993, in Los Angeles.

SEESEL ANN JOHNSON

The Internet Movie Data Base, has Seesel being born in Los Angeles, California, on December 28, 1920. This same source credits Johnson with roles in five films, two of which are B-westerns. She appeared with Tom Mix in RIDERS OF THE PURPLE SAGE ('25) and with Buck Jones in DURAND OF THE BADLANDS ('25). IMDB has Seesel in SPARROWS ('26) with Mary Pickford, FORBIDDEN ('32) with Adolphe Menjou and Barbara Stanwyck, and in TRUE CONFESSION ('37) with Carole Lombard, Fred MacMurray, and John Barrymore. The AMERICAN FILM IN-STITUTE CATALOG has Johnson in one additional picture, YOUTH WILL BE SERVED ('40) with Jane Withers in the lead role. What happened to Seesel Ann is one more of life's mysteries.

PAUL JORDAN

The Internet Movie Data Base credits Paul Jordan with two "Kid Kowboy" roles in 1950. Both are in westerns starring Don "Red" Barry, GUNFIRE and BORDER RANGERS. IMDB'S only other entry for Jordan is to credit him with a part in a film 50 year later, NOSTRADAMUS ('00). *Maybe, but doubt it.*

BILLY KING

Billy King qualifies as a "Kid Kowboy" for his four supporting roles in "Hopalong Cassidy" oaters, as he appeared with William Boyd and Gabby Hayes in HOPALONG RIDES AGAIN ('37), TEXAS TRAIL ('37), HEART OF ARIZONA ('38), and PRIDE OF THE WEST ('38).

King was born on December 11, 1932, in New Mexico. He died in Stanislaus County, California, on December 14, 1972.

ANNABELLE MAGNUS

Annabelle Magnus shared the lead role with Buzz Barton in ORPHANS OF THE SAGE ('28). One review writer was most kind to Miss Magnus, saying, "...played with a twelve-year-old boy and a twelve-year-old girl in the leading roles...The girl, Annabelle Magnus, is a find. FBO should team her with Barton again." Apparently, neither FBO, nor anyone else, was listening because Annabelle never played another "Kid Kowboy" role, nor much of anything else. The *American Film Institute Catalog of Feature Films* lists only two other film credits for Magnus: she appeared in LOVEY MARY ('26) with Bessie Love, and in a film titled HIS DOG ('27). Annabelle appeared in at least one short subject as evidenced by a photo in the author's collection showing her with a group of juvenile players in a scene from a 1927 comedy, WILD PUPPIES.

GREGORY MARSHALL

Gregory Marshall played the young son of Bob Steele in BANDITS OF DARK CANYON ('47). Marshall, who has 21 film credits during his 12 years as a child actor, made his early appearances under the name of Gregory Muradian, probably his true surname. His "Kid Kowboy" credits are limited to his role with Allan Lane and Bob Steele in BANDITS OF DARK CANYON and TWO-GUN MARSHAL ('53) with Guy Madison and Andy Devine, a feature edited from three television episodes of "Wild Bill Hickok."

Marshall's film debut was in THE STRANGE AFFAIR OF UNCLE HARRY ('45) with George Sanders and Ella Rains. Among his other non-western credits are STRANGE CONFESSIONS and HOUSE OF DRACULA ('45) with Lon Chaney, Jr., ROUGHLY SPEAKING ('45) with Jack Carson, CAPTAIN EDDIE ('45) with Fred MacMurray, NIGHT AND DAY ('46) with Cary Grant, THAT'S MY MAN ('46) with Don Ameche, THE BRIDE WORE BOOTS ('46) with Barbara Stanwyck, JOAN OF ARC ('48) with Ingrid Bergman, ADVENTURES IN BALTIMORE ('40) with Shirley Temple, THE FULLER BRUSH GIRL ('50) with Lucille Ball, THE BLUE VEIL ('51) with Jane Wyman, AT SWORD'S POINT ('52) with Cornell Wilde, WASHINGTON STORY ('52) with Van Johnson, and TANGANYIKA ('54) with Van Heflin. He closed out a fairly extensive juvenile acting career with a role in TEENAGE THUNDER ('57). Marshall spent two years, 1953-55, as a cast member on the television series, "The Life of Riley."

BRUCE NORMAN

Bruce Norman, sometimes billed as B. G. Norman, is credited with two roles as a "Kid Kowboy." He had appearances with Allan Lane in SUNDOWN IN SANTA FE ('48) and in THE MARSHAL'S DAUGHTER ('53) with Hoot Gibson. Norman made guest appearances twice on television's "The Gene Autry Show."

BILLY O'BRIEN

"Kid Kowboy" Billy O'Brien began his film career with a role in the serial SIGN OF THE WOLF ('31) supporting Virginia Brown Faire and Joe Bonomo. O'Brien's lone western film credit appears to be with John Wayne in WEST OF THE DIVIDE ('34). Non-westerns in which he is credited include THE POWER AND THE GLORY ('33) with Spencer Tracy, and TRUE CONFESSIONS ('37) with Fred MacMurray and Carole Lombard.

JANINE PERREAU

Janine Perreau, younger sister of "Kid Kowboys" Peter Miles and Gigi Perreau, is the third member of her family to appear in a juvenile support role in western films. She was born on October 19, 1942, in Los Angeles.

Janine was part of the cast of THE REDHEAD AND THE COWBOY ('50) with Glenn Ford. Janine's non-western credits during a career that spanned the years 1947-1954, included roles in SONG OF LOVE ('47) with Katharine Hepburn, THE RED DANUBE ('49) with Walter Pidgeon, NEVER A DULL MOMENT ('50) with Fred MacMurray, WEEK-END WITH FATHER ('51) with Van Heflin, M ('51) with David Wayne, THREE FOR BEDROOM C ('52) with Gloria Swanson, INVADERS FROM MARS ('53) with Helena Carter, and THE SHANGHAI STORY ('54) with Ruth Roman. She was also a guest on an episode of television's "Adventures of Superman" in 1952.

DUNCAN RICHARDSON

In his ten years as a child actor, Duncan Richardson had a "Kid Kowboy" role in GUNMEN OF ABILENE ('50) with Allan Lane. His non-western films commenced with THE SEA OF GRASS ('47) with Spencer Tracy and Katharine Hepburn, and came to a close with SOMETHING OF VALUE ('57) with Rock Hudson. During this time frame, he managed roles in THIS TIME FOR KEEPS ('47) with Esther Williams and Jimmy Durante, MY DREAM IS YOURS ('49) with Jack Carson and Doris Day, THREE CAME HOME ('50) with Claudette Colbert, THREE SECRETS ('50) with Eleanor Parker, THE PRIDE OF MARYLAND ('51) with Frankie Darro, WHITE LIGHTNING ('53), and THE GLASS WEB ('53) with Edward G. Robinson. Richardson is also credited with a television guest role on "The Adventures of Champion."

Richardson was born on November 8, 1942, in Kentucky. He died in Los Angeles on December 10, 1985.

TOMMY RYAN

Thomas "Tommy" Ryan was born in Ohio on March 31, 1926. In a decade as a child actor, Tommy Ryan had "Kid Kowboy" roles in one oater and one serial. He teamed up with Gene Autry in PRAIRIE MOON ('38) and appeared with George Stewart in the 1947 chapterplay, SON OF ZORRO. Tommy's first film was TENTH AVENUE KID ('37) with Bruce Cabot. Included among his 18 credits are several films starring James Gleason: MY WIFE'S RELATIVES ('39), SHOULD HUSBANDS WORK? ('39), THE COVERED TRAILER ('39), MONEY TO BURN ('39), GRANDPA GOES TO TOWN ('40), and EARL OF PUDDLESTONE ('40). TOP BANANA ('53) with Phil Silvers was his final credit. In the interim, he had roles in ORPHANS OF THE STREET ('38) with Bob Livingston and June Storey, STREET OF MISSING MEN ('39) with Charles Bickford, MICKEY THE KID ('39) with Bruce Cabot, BALL OF FIRE ('41) with Gary Cooper, THE STRANGE LOVES OF MARTHA IVERS ('46) with Barbara Stanwyck, CALENDAR GIRL ('47) with Jane Frazee, and HIT PARADE OF 1947 ('47) with Eddie Albert. Ryan died in San Francisco on March 25, 1989.

DON STEWART

Don Stewart, sometimes billed as Donald Stewart, was born in Staten Island, New York, on November 12, 1935, and by age seven appeared on his way to a film career as one of the "Kid Kowboys." In 1942 he appeared with Tom Keene in WHERE TRAILS END. This was followed by roles in WILD HORSE STAMPEDE ('43) with Ken Maynard and Hoot Gibson, and ARIZONA WHIRL-WIND ('44) with the trio of Maynard, Gibson, and Bob Steele, with the added bonus of pretty Myrna Dell in the heroine role.

Attempting to find valid information on Don Stewart following his brief film career was complicated by the fact that there were at least three Don Stewarts in the world of entertainment, and writers have confused not only their film careers, but also their biographical facts. The Internet Movie Data Base, has this Don Stewart in a filmography following Don's last credited film role at age 9, and after a hiatus of over 20 years, suddenly credited with numerous television roles, mainly in soap operas, and a myriad of guest television appearances. *Doubtful.*

Don Stewart died in the state of Washington in December 1986.

ANN TODD

Anne Todd Mayfield was born in Denver, Colorado, on August 26, 1931, and began her career in films as Ann Todd with a role in ZAZA ('39) with Claudette Colbert and Herbert Marshall. She later changed her name to Ann E. Todd in order to avoid confusion with the prominent English actress, Ann Todd.

During her days in films, Ann had roles as a "Kid Kowboy" in DESTRY RIDES AGAIN ('39) with Jimmy Stewart and Marlene Dietrich, BRIGHAM YOUNG-FRONTIERSMAN ('40) with Tyrone Power, Linda Darnell and Dean Jagger, BAD MEN OF MISSOURI ('41) with Dennis Morgan and Jane Wyman, and HOMESTEADERS OF PARADISE VALLEY ('47) with Allan Lane and Bobby Blake.

Her non-westerns appearances include DR. EHRLICH'S MAGIC BULLET ('40) with Edward G. Robinson, ALL THIS AND HEAVEN TOO ('40) with Bette Davis and Charles Boyer, BLOOD AND SAND ('41) with Tyrone Power and Linda Darnell, HOW GREEN WAS MY VALLEY ('41) with Walter Pidgeon and Maureen O'Hara, KING'S ROW ('42) with Ronald Reagan, Ann Sheridan and Robert Cummings, PRIDE OF THE MARINES ('45) with John Garfield and Eleanor Parker, and THE JOLSON STORY ('46) with Larry Parks.

Ann was also active in television with credits with "Alcoa Hour," "U. S. Steel Hour," "G. E. Theatre," "Alfred Hitchcock Theatre" and "Playhouse 90," among others.

A note of interest: Ann claims to be a fourth cousin to Mary Todd Lincoln, Abe's bride.

NORMA JEAN WOOTERS

Norma Jean Wooters played "Kid Kowboy" roles in the only two film appearances in which she is credited. She supported Charles Starrett in BADMEN OF THE HILLS ('42) and THE FIGHTING BUCKAROO ('43).

While no biographical information could be found for Norma Jean, the author suspects that she may have been a sister of another "Kid Kowboy." Mary Lee's surname was Wooters, and Mary did have two sisters.

BIBLIOGRAPHY

Literally hundreds of sources, books, magazines, and periodicals, were reviewed in an effort to obtain information for this book. It was a frustrating task attempting to find actual and accurate biographical information on many of the players. In those few sources where information was located, dates and places of birth and filmographies, were often in error. Information as to parents, siblings, education, marriages, children, grandchildren, occupations after films, and retirement years were obtained largely through personal contacts with surviving players, a few of the truly dedicated western film historians, and from death certificates. A few of the sources listed below offered some information necessary for the success of this book, while others contributed photos of the players. My thanks to the following for whatever role they played in the search for information on the "Kid Kowboys."

Brockman, Alfred. *The Movie Book The 1930's.* Crescent Books, 1987.

Copeland, Bobby. *B-Western Boot Hill.* Empire Publishing,1999.

Copeland, Bobby. *Trail Talk.* Empire Publishing, 1996.

Drake, Oliver. *Written, Produced & Directed by Oliver Drake.* The Outlaw Press, 1990.

Dye, David. *Child and Youth Actors.* McFarland, 1988.

Hardy, Phil. *The Western.* William Morrow and Company, 1983.

Holland, Ted. *B Western Actors Encyclopedia.* McFarland, 1989.

Kietzer, Norman. Editor, *Westerns and Serials,* # 1-43.

King, Bob. Editor, *Classic Images,* # 1-327.

Lahue, Kalton C. *Winners of the West.* A. S. Barnes and Company, 1970.

Lahue, Kalton C. *Riders of the Range.* Castle Books, 1973.

Lamparski, Richard. *Whatever Became Of...?.* Crown Publishers, # 1-11.

McClure and Jones. *Western Films—Heroes, Heavies and Sagebrush.* A. S. Barnes and Company, 1972.

Magers, Boyd. *Western Clippings* # 1-49 (1994-2002).

Magers, Boyd and Fitzgerald, Michael. *Ladies of the Western.* McFarland, 2002.

Mathis, Jack. *Republic Confidential—The Players.* Jack Mathis Advertising, 1992.

Momber, Colin, Editor, *Wrangler's Roost.* Bristol, England.

Nareau, Bob. *Bob Steele—Stars and Support Players.* 1997.

Nareau, Bob. *Those "B" Western Cowboy Heroes Who Rode the Hollywood Range with Bob Steele.* 1999.

Quinlan, Davis. *Quinlan's Illustrated Directory of Film Stars.* Hippocrene Books, 1986.

Ragan, David. *Who's Who in Hollywood.* Arlington House, 1976.

Rainey, Buck. *The Life and Films of Buck Jones—The Silent Era.* The World of Yesterday, 1988.

Rainey, Buck. *The Life and Films of Buck Jones—The Sound Era.* The World of Yesterday, 1991.

Rainey, Buck. *Sweethearts of the Sage.* McFarland, 1992.

Rainey, Buck. *Heroes of the Range.* The World of Yesterday, 1987.

Rainey, Buck. *Serials and Series—A World Filmography—1912-1956.* McFarland, 1999.

Reyes, Luis and Rubie, Peter. *Hispanics in Hollywood.* Garland Publishing, 1994.

Rothel, David. *Those Great Cowboy Sidekicks.* Empire Publishing, 2001.

Watson, Coy, Jr. *The Keystone Kid.* Santa Monica Press, 2001.

ABOUT THE AUTHOR

Bob Nareau was born in Keene, New Hampshire. Early in life, his main interests were movie cowboys and sports. Later on, he discovered girls.

It was during the era that one must "collect" three empty milk bottles to cash in at the local store if he wanted to attend the Saturday matinee and have some penny candy.
Bob's first attempt at creative writing was thwarted by his seventh grade teacher who had assigned him after school to write 50 times, the poem:

> A wise old owl sat in an oak,
> The more he saw, the less he spoke,
> The less he spoke, The more he heard,
> Why can't I be like that bird?

Hand aching, after number 50, he added, "Because I have no feathers." This resulted in 50 more times of writing the poem and put a damper on his thirst to write.

Following the attack on Pearl Harbor, Bob enlisted in the U.S. Navy and spent the next 38 months in bell-bottomed pants and a white hat. Following the war, he attended Columbia University in New York City, where he graduated with the degrees Bachelor of Science, Master of Arts, and completed work on an Education Doctorate. It was at Columbia that Bob had his first contact with the magic of the world of films. Contacted by one Boris Kaplan, a talent scout for Paramount Pictures, he was offered a chance for stardom. Still not too smart, he declined.

Nareau's first job after college was coaching at a school in the Sacramento, California, area. Following two successful years, a new elementary school was opened in the district, and he was appointed principal. Five years of writing articles for various educational journals on programs he instigated, and coping with the woes of 22 women teachers convinced him to move on. For his efforts, Bob was awarded a California Congress of Parents and Teacher Award as Man of the Year.

He then opened his own swimming and tennis club in Carmichael, California, acting as the teaching professional, while attending evening classes at University of Pacific School of Law. Graduating from law school with both a Bachelor and Doctorate of Law, he opened a law practice in San Diego County where for several years he had the largest criminal law defense practice in the County. During this tenure, Nareau managed to change the laws a dozen times in the appellate and supreme courts. He was admitted to practice and argued in the Supreme Court of the United States.

It was during Bob's days as an attorney that he had his second contact with the world of the cinema. He was appointed County Chairman for the election campaign of Hollywood actor Ronald Reagan for governor of California. The campaign was a success and eventually the movie cowboy went on to even bigger things.

The urge to write continued during Bob's practice of law and resulted in articles in various law journals. After many years as a criminal defense attorney, he realized that his work was resulting in putting back on the streets many whom he knew in his heart belonged locked up. He sold his practice and moved with his wife Greta, to the beautiful Island of Kauai in the state of Hawaii, where along with ample beach time, he taught law in the University of Hawaii system.

Today, retired, he, Greta, and granddaughter "Punky" spend their days between attending film festivals "existing" in Arizona, and "living" on Kauai, Hawaii.

Bob Nareau's other books include *The Real Bob Steele and a Man Called "Brad," The Films of Bob Steele, Bob Steele: Stars and Support Players, Bob Steele: His 'Reel' Women, Those "B" Western Cowboy Heroes Who Rode the Hollywood Range with Bob Steele*, and *Bits and Spurs: "B" Western Trivia*.

Bob, "Punky," and Greta Nareau

A LAST WORD BEFORE HITTING THE TRAIL . . .

In art form, here is a final word from Sammy McKim. Sam loves the fans who remember him from his movie acting days, and he was pleased to be inolved in the production of this book.

More Great Western Books available from Empire Publishing...

SILENT HOOFBEATS
by Bobby J. Copeland

A Salute to the Horses and Riders of the Bygone B-Western Era

A beautiful book saluting the great and beautiful horses of the Saturday matinee Westerns! They are all here—Trigger, Champion, Black Jack, Topper and all the rest. Not only is this a book about the horses, but it also contains extensive commentary by the cowboy heroes. And, it is loaded with wonderful photographs.

You will learn many of horses' backgrounds, how they were obtained by the cowboys, and incidents and accidents that happened while filming.

You will also learn which cowboy
...broke his arm when he fell from his
  horse and had to be replaced by another star.
...cried when his horse died.
...said horses were stupid
...beat his horses until they screamed.
...had his horse buried, instead of stuffed, because it was cheaper.
Plus...many more interesting and revealing items.

$20.00
(+ $2.00 s/h)

TRAIL TALK
by Bobby J. Copeland

Bobby Copeland has become a well-versed Western writer in recent years. His down-to-earth style appeals to most every fan.

* IT'S A WESTERN STAR QUOTE BOOK *
Hundreds and Hundreds of Quotes from Your Favorite Cowboys and Cowgirls.

IT'S A WESTERN MOVIE TRIVIA BOOK
You Will Learn...
• What member of TV's "Gunsmoke" was Rex Allen's cousin.
• Who told the studio that the Lone Ranger role was stupid.
• What famous cowboy star divorced his wife and married his mother-in-law.
• Much, much more!

* IT'S A WESTERN MOVIE HISTORY BOOK *
• It informs who were the top 10 money makers from 1936-1954.
• The real names of Cowboys & Cowgirls.
• What America meant to John Wayne
• And more!

ONLY
$12.50
(+ $2.00 s/h)

BILL ELLIOTT: The Peaceable Man
by Bobby J. Copeland

* UNLIKE ANYTHING EVER PRODUCED ON BILL ELLIOTT*

• Wild Bill Elliott
• Bill Elliott in the Comics
• Bill Elliott's Personal Life
• Popularity Ranking of Bill Elliott
• Bill Elliott's Obituary
• They Knew Bill Elliott
• Bill Elliott's Principal Sidekicks
• Bill Elliott and His Horses
• The Real Wild Bill vs. The Reel Wild Bills
• They're Talking about Bill Elliott
• The Starring and Non-Starring Films of Bill Elliott

$15.00
(+ $2.00 s/h)

EMPIRE PUBLISHING, INC. • PO BOX 717 • MADISON, NC 27025 • PH 336-427-5850 • FAX 336-427-7372

122

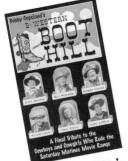

B-WESTERN BOOT HILL

A Final Tribute to the Cowboys and Cowgirls
Who Rode the Saturday Matinee Movie Range

by Bobby j. Copeland

$15.00
(+ $2.00 s/h)

NEWLY REVISED AND UPDATED! Now includes the obituaries of Rex Allen, Dale Evans, Walter Reed, Clayton Moore, and others. ***You asked for it—now here it is . . . an extensively updated version of B-WESTERN BOOT HILL. (The first printing sold out!) An easy reference guide with hundreds of new entries, updates, and revisions. If you've worn out your original BOOT HILL, or are looking for a more complete B-Western reference book, this is the book for you!***

* 1000+ ENTRIES *
The Most Complete List Ever Assembled of Birth Dates, Death Dates, and Real Names of Those Beloved B-Western Performers.

* IT'S A LITERARY MILESTONE *
Bobby Copeland has produced a literary milestone which surely will rank at the top among those important Western film history books printed within the past 30 years. *Richard B. Smith, III*

* OBITUARIES AND BURIAL LOCATIONS *
Through the years, Bobby Copeland has collected actual obituaries of hundreds of B-Western heroes, heavies, helpers, heroines and sidekicks. Also included is a listing of actual burial locations of many of the stars.

* MANY PHOTOS THROUGHOUT *

ROY BARCROFT: King of the Badmen
by Bobby J. Copeland

A WONDERFUL BOOK ABOUT A GREAT CHARACTER ACTOR

In this book, you will find:
· A detailed biography
· Foreword by Monte Hale
· How he selected the name "Roy Barcroft"
· Letters and comments by Roy
· Roy's views about his co-workers
· Co-workers' comments about Roy
· Roy's fans speak out
· Other writers' opinions of Roy Barcraft
· Filmography

$15.00
(+ $2.00 s/h)

CHARLIE KING
We called him "Blackie"
by Bobby J. Copeland

Who was the "baddest" of the badmen?

Many will say it was Charlie King.

This book is a salute to Charles "Blackie" King— one of the premiere B-Western badmen.

Includes:
· The most comprehensive information ever printed on "Blackie"
· The truth about Charlie's death... including his death certificate
· Comments by noted Western film historians
· Remarks by co-workers
· Writers' opinions of Charlie's acting and his career
· Cowboys with whom he worked
· Studios that employed him
· Filmography
· Many photos
· Much, much more

ONLY $15.00
(+ $2.00 s/h)

EMPIRE PUBLISHING, INC. • PO BOX 717 • MADISON, NC 27025 • PH 336-427-5850 • FAX 336-427-7372

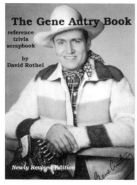
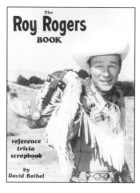

124

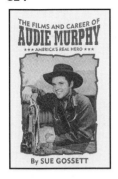

THE FILMS AND CAREER OF
AUDIE MURPHY

by Sue Gossett

$18.00
+ $2.00 shipping

A Film-by-film Synopses of this Legendary Hollywood Star / War Hero

This book reflects all of Audie Murphy's movie career of 44 films. Also included are two of his three made-for-television movies and one episode of his 1961 series, "Whispering Smith."

Along with acting and producing films, Audie's brilliant and well-documented war record is highlighted for those who want a thumb-nail account of what he endured while in the service of his country. This young man was not yet old enough to vote when he was awarded every combat medal for valor this nation had to offer.

Audie Murphy loved country music and expressed himself through the lyrics of dozens of songs, some of which were recorded by famous artists. Some of his poetry and songs are included in a special chapter. Order today!

To celebrate the movie career of Audie Murphy, Sue Gossett and Empire Publishing are delighted to present this volume of *Audie Murphy: Now Showing*. It contains 200+ pages and more than 500 photo illustrations of advertising materials used to promote the 44 films given to Audie's credit. The contents include photos of movie 1-sheet posters, lobby and window display cards, half sheets, publicity items, author's comments, and more. *A must-have for the true Audie Murphy fan!*

Contents include:
• The movie magic of this legendary giant as illustrated via theatrical promotional materials.
• 200+ pages
• More than 500 photo illustrations
• Complete filmography
• Foreign items and testimonials
• Interviews with actors who appeared in his films
• Locations where movies were filmed
• Brief synopsis of each film
• Much more!

Audie Murphy:
NOW SHOWING

by Sue Gossett

Author Sue Gossett is a true Audie Murphy historian, having followed his career since 1954.

$30.00
+ $3.00 shipping

Those Great COWBOY SIDEKICKS
by David Rothel

• 8-1/2 x 11
• 300+ PAGES
• BEAUTIFUL COLOR COVER
• OVER 200 PHOTOS
• **$25.00** (+ $3.00 s/h)

This book features in-depth profiles of such fondly-remembered character actors as George "Gabby" Hayes, Smiley Burnette, Andy Devine, Al "Fuzzy" St. John, Pat Buttram, Max Terhune, Fuzzy Knight, and many other sidekicks of the B-Westerns—thirty-nine in all! Much of *Those Great Cowboy Sidekicks* is told through the reminiscences of the sidekicks themselves and the cowboy stars who enjoyed the company of these often bewhiskered, tobacco-chewing saddle pals. Mr. Rothel provides the reader with the rare opportunity to go behind the scenes to discover the manner in which Western screen comedy was created.

Author David Rothel is a Western film historian who has also written An Ambush of Ghosts, Tim Holt, and Richard Boone, A Knight Without Armor in a Savage Land, among several other titles.

EMPIRE PUBLISHING, INC. • PO BOX 717 • MADISON, NC 27025 • PH 336-427-5850 • FAX 336-427-7372

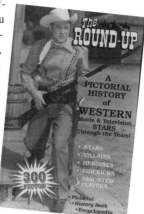

126

RANDOLPH SCOTT
A FILM BIOGRAPHY
by Jefferson Brim Crow, III

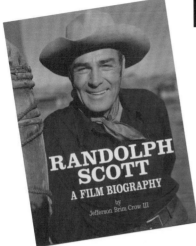

- 8-1/2 x 11
- Beautiful color cover
- Over 250 photographs
- 302 pages
- Softcover

This book contains the only complete biography of this legendary star.

$25⁰⁰
(+ $3⁰⁰ s/h)

WHATEVER HAPPENED TO RANDOLPH SCOTT?

by C. H. Scott

This is not just another book about a movie actor who made it to the glamour and glitz of the Hollywood scene. It is a love story that reveals the respect and admiration of a son for his father. Upon reading this narrative, one will experience growing up in the home of Randolph Scott, through the eyes of his son, Chris. As the reader begins to grieve the loss of one of Hollywood's finest stars, the answer to the question, *Whatever Happened to Randolph Scott?* will fill the heart with hope . . . he lives on in those who loved him. Includes many rare, personal photos.

$12.95
(+ $2⁰⁰ shipping)

MORE COWBOY SHOOTING STARS

by
John A. Rutherford
and
Richard B. Smith, III

Ask for our complete listing of 300+ movie books!

$18.00
(+ $3⁰⁰ shipping)

This is a hardcover reference book that contains almost every Western film produced from 1930 through 1992 — The B's, The A's — they all are included. This reference book has each Western film star listed with each of their films in chronological order. There are 7,267 entries in all with 105 cowboy and cowgirl pictures are within.

Hardcover; 214 pages.

SO YOU WANNA SEE COWBOY STUFF?

The Western Movie/TV Tour Guide

by Boyd Magers

Here's the only complete tour guide ever assembled leading you directly to all the western movie and TV memorabilia as well as filming locations in the entire United States!

From California to Maine you will find:

- Exact filming locations where Roy Rogers, Gene Autry, Hopalong Cassidy, Bill Elliott, John Wayne, "Bonanza", The Durango Kid and all the rest shot their western films. Iverson's Corriganville, Old Tucson, Lone Pine, Sedona, Melody Ranch, Jauregui Ranch, Kernville, Moab, Walker Ranch, Bronson Cave, Monument Valley, Vasquez Rocks, Pioneertown, Big Bear, Kanab.

- Murals, Birthplaces, Monuments, Statues, Parks, Exhibits, Rodeos, Road Markers, Hotels, Bronzes and more!

- The Top Western Museums in the Country—Gene Autry, Roy Rogers, Rex Allen, Will Rogers, John Wayne, Andy Devine, Warner Bros., George Montgomery, Red Ryder, Buddy Roosevelt, Ken Maynard, Tom Mix, James Stewart, Audie Murphy, Tex Ritter, Yakima Canutt.

- Detailed Studio Guides to Republic, Warner Bros., Universal, Monogram.

- Birthplaces, Childhood Homes and Former Residences of Roy Rogers, Hopalong Cassidy, Gail Davis, Tom Mix, William S. Hart, Joel McCrea, Ken Maynard, John Wayne, Dale Evans, Gene Autry, Audie Murphy.

- Detailed Guide to Western Stars on the Hollywood Walk of Fame, Newhall Walk of Stars, Palm Springs Walk of Fame and others.

- How to Find, Visit and See Gower Gulch, Ray "Crash" Corrigan's Grill, Fess Parker's Winery, John Wayne's Wild Goose yacht, Clint Eastwood's Mission Ranch, the Pro Rodeo Hall of Fame, the Lone Ranger's Mask, Hoot Gibson's Rodeo, the John Ford Memorial, Roy Rogers Restaurants, Sky King's Songbird, The Ponderosa "Bonanza" Ranch, Rex Bell's Ranch, the bar used on "Gunsmoke", Buck Jones' Circus Wagon, Railroads and Locomotives used in dozens of westerns.

- Gravesites of John Wayne, Roy Rogers, Gene Autry, Audie Murphy, Hoppy's Topper and others.

- Complete Listing of All the Annual Western Film Festivals!

Written and Extensively Researched Over a Three Year Period by Boyd Magers, Author of WESTERN CLIPPINGS Magazine, WESTERNS WOMEN and LADIES OF THE WESTERN among others. Special Movie Locations Contributions in Association with Noted Authority Tinsley Yarbrough.

- Hardcover; 8-1/2 x 11"
- Glossy Stock throughout
- 264 pages
- Hundreds of photographs

$35⁰⁰
+ $3.00 s/h

EMPIRE PUBLISHING, INC. • PO BOX 717 • MADISON, NC 27025-0717 • PH: 336-427-5850 • FAX 336-427-7372

Other Fine Western Movie Books Available from Empire Publishing, Inc:

ABC's of Movie Cowboys by Edgar M. Wyatt. $5.00.

Audie Murphy: Now Showing by Sue Gossett. $30.00.

Back in the Saddle: Essays on Western Film and Television Actors edited by Garry Yoggy. $24.95.

Bill Elliott, The Peaceable Man by Bobby Copeland. $15.00.

Bits and Spurs: B-Western Trivia by Bob Nareau. $20.00.

Bob Steele, His "Reel" Women by Bob Nareau. $20.00.

Bob Steele, Stars and Support Players by Bob Nareau. $20.00.

B-Western Actors Encyclopedia by Ted Holland. $30.00.

Buster Crabbe, A Self-Portrait as told to Karl Whitezel. $24.95.

B-Western Boot Hill: A Final Tribute to the Cowboys and Cowgirls Who Rode the Saturday Matinee Movie Range (revised edition) by Bobby Copeland. $15.00.

The Cowboy and the Kid by Jefferson Brim Crow, III. $5.90.

Duke, The Life and Image of John Wayne by Ronald L. Davis. $12.95.

The Films and Career of Audie Murphy by Sue Gossett. $18.00.

The Films of the Cisco Kid by Francis M. Nevins, Jr. $19.95.

The Films of Hopalong Cassidy by Francis M. Nevins, Jr. $19.95.

From Pigskin to Saddle Leather: The Films of Johnny Mack Brown by John A. Rutherford. $19.95.

The Gene Autry Reference-Trivia-Scrapbook by David Rothel. $25.00.

The Golden Corral, A Roundup of Magnificent Western Films by Ed Andreychuk. $29.95.

The Hollywood Posse, The Story of a Gallant Band of Horsemen Who Made Movie History by Diana Serra Cary. $16.95.

Hoppy by Hank Williams. $29.95.

In a Door, Into a Fight, Out a Door, Into a Chase, Movie-Making Remembered by the Guy at the Door by William Witney. $32.50.

John Ford, Hollywood's Old Master by Ronald L. Davis. $14.95.

John Wayne—Actor, Artist, Hero by Richard D. McGhee. $25.00.

John Wayne, An American Legend by Roger M. Crowley. $29.95.

Lash LaRue, King of the Bullwhip by Chuck Thornton and David Rothel. $25.00.

Last of the Cowboy Heroes by Budd Boetticher. $32.50.

The Life and Films of Buck Jones, the Silent Era by Buck Rainey. $14.95.

The Life and Films of Buck Jones, the Sound Era by Buck Rainey. $24.95.

More Cowboy Movie Posters by Bruce Hershenson. $20.00.

More Cowboy Shooting Stars by John A. Rutherford and Richard B. Smith, III. $18.00.

The Official TV Western Roundup Book by Neil Summers and Roger M. Crowley. $34.95.

Quiet on the Set, Motion Picture History at the Iverson Movie Location Ranch by Robert G. Sherman. $14.95.

Randolph Scott, A Film Biography by Jefferson Brim Crow, III. $25.00.

Richard Boone: A Knight Without Armor in a Savage Land by David Rothel. $30.00.

Riding the (Silver Screen) Range, The Ultimate Western Movie Trivia Book by Ann Snuggs. $15.00.

Riding the Video Range, The Rise and Fall of the Western on Television by Garry A. Yoggy. $75.00.

The Round-Up, A Pictorial History of Western Movie and Television Stars Through the Years by Donald R. Key. $27.00.

Roy Rogers, A Biography, Radio History, Television Career Chronicle, Discography, Filmography, etc. by Robert W. Phillips. $65.00.

The Roy Rogers Reference-Trivia-Scrapbook by David Rothel. $25.00.

Saddle Gals, A Filmography of Female Players in B-Westerns of the Sound Era by Edgar M. Wyatt and Steve Turner. $10.00.

Saddle Pals: A Complete B-Western Roster of the Sound Era by Garv Towell and Wayne E. Keates. $5.00.

Silent Hoofbeats: A Salute to the Horses and Riders of the Bygone B-Western Era by Bobby Copeland. $20.00.

Singing in the Saddle by Douglas B. Green. $34.95.

The Sons of the Pioneers by Bill O'Neal and Fred Goodwin. $26.95.

So You Wanna See Cowboy Stuff? by Boyd Magers.

Television Westerns Episode Guide by Harris M. Lentz, III. $95.00.

Tex Ritter: America's Most Beloved Cowboy by Bill O'Neal. $21.95.

Those B-Western Cowboy Heroes Who Rode the Hollywood Range with Bob Steele by Bob Nareau. $20.00.

Those Great Cowboy Sidekicks by David Rothel. $25.00.

Those Wide Open Spaces by Hank Williams. $29.95.

Tim Holt by David Rothel. $30.00.

The Tom Mix Book by M. G. "Bud" Norris. $24.95.

Trail Talk, Candid Comments and Quotes by Performers and Participants of The Saturday Matinee Western Films by Bobby Copeland. $12.50.

The Western Films of Sunset Carson by Bob Carman and Dan Scapperotti. $20.00.

Western Movies: A TV and Video Guide to 4200 Genre Films compiled by Michael R. Pitts. $25.00.

Westerns Women by Boyd Magers and Michael G. Fitzgerald. $36.50.

Whatever Happened to Randolph Scott? by C. H. Scott. $12.95.

White Hats and Silver Spurs, Interviews with 24 Stars of Film and Television Westerns of the 1930s-1960s. $38.50.

Add $3.00 shippping/handling for 1st book + $1.00 for each additional book ordered.

Empire Publishing, Inc. • PO Box 717 • Madison, NC 27025-0717 • Ph 336-427-5850